ALSO AVAILABLE:

FISH! Tales:
Real-Life Stories to Help You Transform
Your Workplace and Your Life

FISH! Sticks:
A Remarkable Way to Adapt to
Changing Times and Keep Your Work Fresh

FISH! for Life:
A Remarkable Way to Achieve Your Dreams

**A Proven Way to Boost Morale
and Improve Results**

Stephen C. Lundin, Ph.D., Harry Paul,

and John Christensen

Grateful acknowledgment is made for permission to reprint copyrighted material from the following: *Simple Abundance: A Daybook of Comfort and Joy*, copyright © 1995 by Sarah Ban Breathnach, published by Warner Books. Reprinted by permission of the author; "Faith" from *Where Many Rivers Meet: Poems*, copyright © 1996 by David Whyte, published by Many Rivers Press. Reprinted by permission of the publisher.

First published by Hyperion in 2000
First published in Great Britain in 2001 by Hodder & Stoughton
An Hachette UK company

Reissued in May 2014

1

Copyright © 2000 Stephen C. Lundin, Harry Paul, and John Christensen by arrangement with Hyperion.

The right of Stephen C. Lundin, Harry Paul, and John Christensen to be identified as the Author of the Work has been asserted by them in accordance with the Copyright, Designs and Patents Act 1988.

All rights reserved. No part of this publication may be reproduced, stored in a retrieval system, or transmitted, in any form or by any means without the prior written permission of the publisher, nor be otherwise circulated in any form of binding or cover other than that in which it is published and without a similar condition being imposed on the subsequent purchaser.

All characters in this publication are fictitious and any resemblance to real persons, living or dead, is purely coincidental.

A CIP catalogue record for this title is available from the British Library

ISBN 978 1 444 79280 5

Printed and bound by Clays Ltd, St Ives plc

Hodder & Stoughton policy is to use papers that are natural, renewable and recyclable products and made from wood grown in sustainable forests. The logging and manufacturing processes are expected to conform to the environmental regulations of the country of origin.

Hodder & Stoughton Ltd
338 Euston Road
London NW1 3BH

www.hodder.co.uk

An Update from the Authors

The FISH! Philosophy has helped millions of people in tens of thousands of organizations around the world—from businesses to schools to hospitals—to deliver amazing service, strengthen trust and teamwork, and bring energy and passion to their work.

The beauty of The FISH! Philosophy is that you can apply it to *every* part of your life. It helps you to be more aware of how your choices impact others, and provides a common language that puts everyone on the same page and shifts conversations toward the positive.

A philosophy becomes real when it is lived. Credit for the success of The FISH! Philosophy belongs to the people who have applied it in ways we never could have imagined. Because their stories have taught and inspired us, we have included a few of them in the back

FISH!

of this book so that you can experience some of the amazing ways that people are bringing The FISH! Philosophy to life.

As authors, we are deeply grateful to the millions of people who have read *FISH!* and, most important, put its lessons into action. We dedicate this book to you.

Steve, Harry and John

Foreword

by Ken Blanchard, Ph.D.,
co-author of *The One Minute Manager*

What you have in your hands is a classic tale about transforming your work into your passion. Since its first printing in 2000, *FISH!* has sold more than five million copies in thirty-five languages, making it one of the best-selling business books of all time. It's easy to see why. With captivating storytelling, timeless advice, an easy-to-follow approach, and an inspirational zeal, The FISH! Philosophy is the perfect message for our time.

The story at the heart of *FISH!*—about a woman who transforms her attitude about work and transforms her lifeless workplace into one of energy and fun—grew out of an amazing video John Christensen produced about the fishmongers of the world-famous Pike Place Fish Market in Seattle. Every day the fishmongers wow their customers with extraordinary attentiveness and spirit-lifting antics. Their world-class customer care has made the Pike Place Fish Market some of the most successful 1,200 square feet of retail space in America.

People spend about seventy-five percent of their adult waking time doing work-related activities—getting ready for work, traveling to and from work, working, contemplating work, and decompressing after work. If we spend that much time on that part of our lives, we ought to enjoy it and be energized by it. Sadly, too many people still have a "thank God it's Friday" attitude about work, trading time on the job to satisfy needs elsewhere.

What this timeless book makes clear is that being there for customers and coworkers, choosing to have fun, and making people's day lead to happiness, meaning, and fulfillment. The FISH! Philosophy works for organizations large or small. It's just as effective in the public sector as it is in the private sector. In fact, these powerful tools can liven up life at home as well as at work.

This book is not just about selling fish; it's a love story. Share it with the people in your workplace. Practice the four strategies. Prepare to be amazed by what happens when you tap into the passion, energy, and enthusiasm that are available to every one of us.

LOVING WHAT YOU DO

It is fashionable today to believe that we should not settle for anything less than doing what we love. Write poetry, travel the world on a sailboat, paint—do whatever you love, and the money will follow. We tell ourselves that life is too short to spend our working hours doing anything less than the ideal, and we continue our search for the perfect workplace. The danger is that if our quest for ideal work focuses us on the future, we will miss the amazingly wonderful life that is available today, in this moment.

The fact is that in the real world there are conditions that prevent us from chasing the perfect, ideal job. Many of us have significant responsibilities to family members or to a way of life. For others, a true calling hasn't made itself visible yet. Some of us are under so much stress in our personal lives that there is literally no time or energy to seek a new line of work.

FISH! is a parable, an invented story about finding the deep source of energy, creativity, and passion that exist inside each of us by learning to love what we do, even if at the moment we may not be doing exactly what we love.

Seattle—Monday Morning

It was a wet, cold, dark, dreary, dismal Monday in Seattle, inside and out. The best the meteorologist on Channel 4 could offer was a possible break in the clouds around noon. On days like this Mary Jane Ramirez missed Southern California.

What a roller coaster, she thought, as her mind retraced the past three years. Dan, her husband, had received a great offer from Microrule, and she had been confident she could find a job once they relocated. In just four short weeks they had given notice, packed, moved, and found great day care for their young children, Brad and Stacy. Their house hit the Los Angeles housing market just at the right time and sold immediately. True to her confidence, Mary Jane quickly found a supervisory position in the operations area of First Guarantee Financial, one of Seattle's largest financial institutions.

Dan loved his job at Microrule. When he came home at night he was bursting with energy and full of stories about what a great company it was and the advanced work they were doing. Dan and Mary Jane would frequently put the children to bed and talk well into the evening. As excited as Dan was about his new company, he was always just as interested in her day, wanting to know about her new colleagues and the challenges she was facing in her work life. Anyone watching would easily guess that they were best friends. The spirit of each shone in the presence of the other.

They planned their move to Seattle with great care, anticipating every possible contingency but one. Twelve months after relocating, Dan was rushed to the hospital with a burst aneurysm—"a genetic oddity," they called it—and he died of internal bleeding, never

FISH!

regaining consciousness. There was no warning and no time to say good-bye.

That was two years ago this month. We weren't even in Seattle a full year.

Stopping in mid-thought, with memories flooding her mind, Mary Jane felt a surge of emotion well up inside her. She caught herself. *This is not the time to think about my personal life; the workday is less than half over, and I'm swamped with work.*

First Guarantee Financial

During her three years at First Guarantee, Mary Jane had developed a great reputation as a "can-do" supervisor. She wasn't the first to arrive or the last to leave, but she was extremely productive and efficient.

She was also a good person to work for. She always listened closely to the concerns and ideas of her staff and was well liked and respected in return. It wasn't uncommon for her to cover for someone with a sick child or important appointment. And, as a working manager, she led her department in production. She did this in an easygoing way that rarely generated any tension. Her direct reports and associates enjoyed working with and for her. Mary Jane's small group developed a reputation as a team you could count on.

In sharp contrast, there was a large operations group on the third floor that was often the topic of conversation for the opposite reason. Words like *unresponsive, entitlement, zombie, unpleasant, slow, wasteland*, and *negative* were used frequently to describe this group. It was the group everyone loved to hate. Unfortunately for the company, nearly every department needed to interact with the third floor since they processed most of First Guarantee's transactions. Everyone dreaded any contact with the operations group.

Supervisors swapped stories about the latest fiasco on the third floor. Those who visited the third floor described it as a place so dead that it sucked the life right out of you. Mary Jane remembered the laughter when one of the other managers said that he deserved a Nobel Prize. When she asked what he meant, he said, "I think I may have discovered life on the third floor." Everyone roared.

Then, much to her surprise, a few weeks later, Mary Jane was offered a promotion to manager of the operations group on the third floor of First Guarantee, a job she cautiously and somewhat reluctantly accepted.

FISH!

While the company had great hopes for her, she had major reservations about her new position. She had been comfortable in her present job—and her willingness to take risks had been much higher before Dan's death. The group she had been supervising had been with her during the rough days after Dan's death, and she had felt a strong bond with them. It would be hard to leave people who had shared so much of themselves during such dark times.

Mary Jane was acutely aware of the terrible reputation of the third floor. In fact, if it hadn't been for all of the unforeseen expenses of Dan's hospitalization, she probably would have turned down the promotion and pay raise. So here she was, on the infamous third floor: the third person to have the job in the last two years.

The Third Floor

"Thank God it's Friday," Mary Jane thought as she looked at her email inbox. Five weeks into the job, she still struggled to understand the work and the people on the third floor. While mildly surprised that she liked many of the people who worked on three, she had quickly realized that the third floor deserved its

FISH!

reputation. She had observed Bob, a five-year veteran on the third floor, letting the phone ring seven times before purposely breaking the connection by unplugging the cord. She had overheard Martha describing how she handled those in the company who "hassled" her to do her processing faster—she deleted their emails "by mistake." Every time Mary Jane went into the break room there was someone dozing at the table.

Most mornings the phones rang unanswered for ten to fifteen minutes after the official start of the day because the staff was still arriving. When questioned, the excuses were both abundant and lame. Everything was in slow motion. It was clear that the "zombie" description of the third floor was definitely deserved. Mary Jane did not have a clue what to do, only the knowledge and conviction that she must do something and do it soon.

That night after the kids were asleep, she had tried to work out her situation by writing in her journal:

> It may have been cold and dreary outside today, but the view from my internal office window made dreary sound like a compliment. There was no energy there. At times I find it hard to

believe there are living human beings on three. It takes a baby shower or a wedding for anyone to come alive. They never get excited about anything that's actually happening at work.

I have thirty employees for whom I am responsible and for the most part they do a slow, short day's work for a low day's pay. Many of them have done the same slow day's work in the same way for years and are totally bored. They seem to be good people, but whatever spark they may have once had, they have lost. The culture of the department is such a powerful and depressing force that new people quickly lose their spark as well. When I walk among the cubicles it feels like all the oxygen has been sucked right out of the air. I can hardly breathe.

Last week I discovered four clerks who were still not using the new software installed here two years ago. They said they liked doing it the old way. I wonder how many other surprises are in store for me.

I suppose many back-room operations are like this. Not much here to get excited about, just lots of transactions that need to be processed.

FISH!

> But it doesn't have to be like this. I must find a way to convey how crucial our work is to the company. Our work allows others to serve the company's customers.
>
> Although our work may be a critical part of the big picture, it happens behind the scenes and is basically taken for granted. It's an invisible part of the organization and would never appear on the company's radar screen if it wasn't so bad. And believe me, it is bad.
>
> It is not a love for this work that brings any of us to this department. I'm not the only person with money problems on this floor. Many of the women and one of the men are also single parents. Jack's ailing father just moved in with him. Bonnie and her husband now have two grandchildren as full-time residents. The big three are why we are here: salary, security, and benefits.

Mary Jane pondered the last sentence she had written in her journal. Back-room operations had always been lifetime positions. The pay was adequate, and the jobs were secure. When she arrived at the office Monday morning, she looked at the rows of cubicles and desks outside her office, and began to formulate some questions. "Does my staff know that the security they cherish might be just an illusion? Do they realize the extent to which market forces are reshaping this industry? Do they understand that we will all need to change in order for this company to compete in a rapidly consolidating financial services market? Are they aware that if we don't change we will eventually find ourselves looking for other employment?"

She knew the answers. No. No. No. No. Her staff members were set in their ways. They had been left alone in the back room far too long. They were just doing their jobs and hoping that retirement would come before change. And what about herself? Was her view that different?

The ringing phone pulled her back into the present. The call was followed by a sixty-minute blur of "firefighting." First, she found out that an important client file was missing and it was rumored to have last been seen on the third floor. Next, someone from another department was so sick and tired of being put on hold she came to the third floor in person and was creating an unpleasant scene. At least there was some energy to work with. Then someone from legal was disconnected

FISH!

three times in a row. And one of the many staff members out ill today had an important project due. After the last fire of the morning was extinguished, Mary Jane reached for her lunch and headed for the door.

The Toxic Energy Dump

Mary Jane had gotten into the habit of leaving the building for lunch every day since she started working on the third floor. She knew if she joined her colleagues in the cafeteria, they would be doing what they always did, discussing the sins of the company and moaning about the third floor. It was now too personal and much too depressing to listen to their complaints. She needed some fresh air.

Most of the time she strolled down the hill to eat lunch at the waterfront. There, while nibbling on a bagel, she would gaze at the water or watch the tourists mill around the little shops. It was a tranquil setting, and Puget Sound provided her some contact with the natural world.

Back from lunch, Mary Jane had made it just two cubicles from her office when she heard the distinct sound of her phone ringing. *It could be the day care*, she thought. *Stacy did have a runny nose this morning.* So she raced back to her office, picking up the phone on the fourth ring. "This is Mary Jane Ramirez," she gasped.

"Mary Jane, this is Bill."

Oh boy, what now, she wondered, as she listened to the voice of her new boss. Bill was another reason she had thought twice about taking the job on three. He had a reputation as a real SOB. As far as she could tell, his reputation was deserved. He would issue commands, cut you off midsentence, and had an annoying habit of asking about the status of projects in a patronizing way. "Mary Jane, are you staying on top of the Stanton project?" As if she didn't have a clue. Mary Jane was the third manager in two years, and she was beginning to understand that it wasn't just the problems with the people on three, it was also Bill.

"I've just come out of an all-morning meeting with the leadership group, and I want to meet with you this afternoon."

"Sure, Bill. Is there a problem?"

"The leadership is convinced that we're in for some tough times and in order to survive, we will need the best from everyone. More productivity from the same employees, or we start making changes. We talked

FISH!

about the corrosive effect of a few departments, where the energy and morale are so low that it pulls everyone down."

A feeling of dread descended upon Mary Jane. "The boss went to one of those touchy-feely conferences on spirit in the workplace, and he's all fired up. I don't think it's fair to single out the third floor, but he seems to believe the third floor is the biggest problem."

"He singled out the third floor?"

"Not only did he single out the third floor, but he had a special name for it. He called it a 'toxic energy dump.' I don't want one of my departments called a toxic energy dump! It's unacceptable! It's embarrassing."

"A toxic energy dump?"

"Yes. And the boss really grilled me on what I'm doing about it. I told him I shared his concern and that I brought you in to solve the problem. He told me he wants to be kept informed of the progress. So, have you solved it yet?"

Have I solved it yet?! I only took the job five weeks ago!
"Not yet," she said.

"Well, you have to speed things up, Mary Jane. If you're not up to it I need to know so I can make the appropriate changes. The boss is absolutely convinced we all need more energy, passion, and spirit on the job. I'm not sure why the third floor needs passion and energy. The stuff you do there is not rocket science. Anyway, just a head's up that I'll be setting up this meeting for this week or next."

"Okay, fine."

Bill must have heard the frustration in her voice. "Now don't get upset, Mary Jane. You just get to work on this."

He really is hard to take, she thought as she hung up the phone. *Don't get upset! He is my boss, and the problem is real. But what a jerk.*

A Change in Routine

Mary Jane's mind was ablaze as she moved toward the elevators later that day. After that stressful call with Bill, she needed a little fresh air and decided to take a quick walk. Rather than heading down the hill to the waterfront as usual, she impulsively turned right on First Street. The words *toxic energy dump* played over and over in her head.

Toxic energy dump! What next? She was walking along First Street when a small voice inside her head whispered, "The toxic energy is what you hate most about the third floor. Something needs to happen."

FISH!

Mary Jane's impulsive stroll down First Street took her to a part of town that was new to her. Sounds of pealing laughter caught her attention and she made her way over to the lively public market. She had heard about the famous Pike Place Market, but with her tight financial situation and two young children, it wasn't a place she'd found her way to.

As she turned and walked down Pike Place, she saw that a large crowd of well-dressed people was clustered around one of the fish markets, and everyone was laughing. At first she felt herself resisting the laughter, dwelling on the seriousness of her predicament. She almost turned away. Then a voice in her head said, "I could use a good laugh," and she moved closer. One of the fish guys yelled out, "Good afternoon, yogurt dudes!" Dozens of well-dressed people then hoisted yogurt cups into the air. *My goodness*, she thought. *What have I stumbled upon?*

The World-Famous Pike Place Fish Market

Was that a fish flying through the air? She wondered if her eyes were playing tricks on her; then it happened again. One of the workers—they were distinctive in their white aprons and black rubber boots—picked up a large fish, threw it twenty feet to the raised counter, and shouted, "One salmon flying away to Minnesota." Then all the other workers repeated in unison, "One salmon flying away to Minnesota." The guy behind the counter made an unbelievable one-handed catch, then bowed his head to the people applauding his skill. The energy was remarkable.

To her right, another worker was playfully teasing a small boy by making a large fish move its mouth as if it were talking. A slightly older fish guy with thinning gray hair was walking around shouting, "Questions, questions, answers to any questions about fish!" A young worker at the cash register was juggling crabs. Two card-carrying members of AARP were laughing uncontrollably as their fish-guy salesman carried on a conversation with the fish they had chosen. The place was wild. She could feel herself relax as she enjoyed the spectacle.

She looked at the people holding the yogurt cups in the air and thought, *Office workers. Do they really buy fish at lunch or do they just come to watch the action?*

Mary Jane was unaware that one of the fish guys had noticed her in the crowd. There was something about her curiosity and seriousness that caused him to walk over.

FISH!

"What's the matter? Don't you have any yogurt?" She looked around and saw a handsome young man with long, curly black hair. He was looking at her intently, a big smile on his face.

"Um, no," she stammered. "I just came here on a quick break from work."

"Have you been here before?"

"No. I usually go down to the waterfront for lunch."

"I can understand that—it's peaceful by the water. Not very peaceful here, that's for sure. So what brings you here today?"

Off to her right one of the fish guys, looking lost, was shouting, "Who wants to buy a fish?" Another was teasing a young woman. A crab sailed over Mary Jane's head. "Six crabs flying away to Montana," someone shouted. "Six crabs flying away to Montana," they all repeated. A fish guy wearing a wool cap was dancing behind the cash register. It was a controlled madhouse all around her, like the rides at the state fair, only better. But the fish guy at her side didn't seem at all distracted. He was pleasantly and patiently waiting for her response. *My goodness*, she thought. *He actually seems interested in my answer. But I'm not going to tell a total stranger about my troubles at work.* Then she did just that.

FISH!

His name was Lonnie, and he listened attentively to her description of the third floor. He didn't flinch when one of the flying fish hit a rope and smacked the ground right beside them. He listened closely as she described the many employee problems she had identified. When she finished telling her story, she looked at Lonnie and asked, "So what do you think about my toxic energy dump?"

"That's quite a story. I've worked in some pretty dreary places myself. In fact this place used to be pretty crappy. What do you notice about the market now?"

"The noise, the action, the energy," she said, without a moment's hesitation.

"And how do you like all this energy?"

"I love it," she replied. "I really love it!"

"Me, too. I'm spoiled for life. I don't think I could work in a typical market after experiencing this. As I mentioned, the market didn't start this way. It, too, was an energy dump for many years. Then we decided to change things—and this is the result. Would energy like this make a difference with your group?"

"It sure would. It's what we need at the dump," she said, smiling.

"I'd be happy to describe what I think makes this

fish market different. Who knows; you might get some ideas."

"But, but we don't have anything to throw! We have boring work to do. Most of us..."

"Slow down. It's not just about throwing fish. Of course your business is different, and it sounds like you have a serious challenge facing you. I'd like to help. What if you could find your own way to apply some of the lessons we learned while becoming the world-famous Pike Place Fish Market? Wouldn't the possibility of an energized department make it worthwhile for you to learn those lessons?"

"Yes. For sure! But why would you do this for me?"

"Being a part of this little fish-market community and experiencing what you see here have made a big difference in my life. I won't bore you with the personal details, but my life was a real mess when I took this job. Working here has literally saved me. It may sound a little sappy, but I believe I have an obligation to seek out and find ways to demonstrate my gratitude for this life I enjoy. You made that easy for me by telling me about your problem. I really believe you can find some of your answers here. We've created a lot of great energy." As he said the word *energy*, a crab sailed by and someone

FISH!

shouted with a Texas twang, "Five crabs flying away to Wisconsin." A chorus echoed, "Five crabs flying away to Wisconsin."

"Fair enough," she answered, laughing out loud. "If the fish market has anything, it has energy. It's a deal." She looked at her watch and realized she would have to walk fast in order to get back to work within the lunch hour. She had no doubt her arrivals and departures were being clocked by her staff.

Lonnie caught her glance and said, "Hey, why don't you come back for your lunch break tomorrow—and bring two yogurts."

He turned and immediately began helping a young man in a Vikings jacket understand the difference between a Copper River salmon and a King salmon.

Return Visit

At lunchtime on Tuesday she walked quickly down First Street to the market. Lonnie must have been watching for her; he immediately emerged from the crowd and directed her down a ramp past the T-shirt concession.

"There are some tables at the end of the hall," he said, and led the way to a small glass-enclosed room

FISH!

with a great view of the harbor and Puget Sound. Lonnie ate a bagel and the yogurt Mary Jane brought him while she ate her yogurt and asked about the workings of the fish market. Fishmongering really didn't sound very appealing after Lonnie told her about a typical day; this made the attitude of the workers at the Pike Place Fish Market all the more impressive.

"It would seem that your work and my work have more in common than I thought," she said, after Lonnie described the tedious tasks that needed to be conducted each day.

Lonnie looked up, "Really?"

"Yes, most of the work my staff does can be mundane and repetitious, to say the least. It's important work, however. We never see a customer, but if we make a mistake, the customer is upset and we receive a lot of criticism. If we do our work well, no one notices. In general, the work is boring. You've taken boring work and made the way you do it interesting. I find that fascinating."

"Have you ever considered the fact that any work can be boring to the person who has to do it? Some of the yogurt dudes travel all over the world for business. It sounds pretty exciting to me, but they tell me it gets old fast. I guess given the right conditions, any job can be dull."

"I agree with that. When I was a teenager I had a chance to do a job many teenage girls often dream about: I was signed up by a modeling agency. But by the end of the first month I was bored to tears. It was almost all just standing around, waiting. Or take newscasters. Many of them do nothing other than read other people's text. That sounds boring, also—at least to me."

"OK. If we agree that any job can be boring, can we agree that any job can be performed with energy and enthusiasm?"

"I'm not sure. Can you give me an example?"

"That's easy. Walk around the market and look at the other fish shops. They don't get it. They are, what was the phrase you used...toxic energy dumps. The way they approach their work is really good for *our* business. I've told you the Pike Place Fish Market used to be like them. Then we discovered an amazing thing. *There is always a choice about the way you do your work, even if there is not a choice about the work itself.* That was the biggest lesson we learned in building the world-famous Pike Place Fish Market. *We can choose the attitude we bring to our work.*"

FISH!

CHOOSE YOUR ATTITUDE

Mary Jane pulled out a notepad and began writing:

> There is always a choice about
> the way you do your work,
> even if there is not
> a choice about the work itself.

Then she thought about the words she had just written, and asked, "Why wouldn't you have a choice about the work itself?"

"Good point. You can always quit your job, and so in that sense you have a choice about the work you do. But it might not be a smart thing to do given your responsibilities and other factors. That's what I mean by choice. On the other hand, you always have a choice about the attitude you bring to the job."

Lonnie continued, "Let me tell you about my grandmother. She always brought love and a smile to her work. All of us grandkids wanted to help in the kitchen because washing dishes with Grandma was so much fun. In the process a great deal of kitchen wisdom was dispensed. We kids were given something truly precious, a caring adult.

"I realize now that my grandmother didn't love dishwashing. She *brought* love to dishwashing, and her spirit was infectious.

"Likewise, my buddies and I realized that each day when we come to the fish market we bring an attitude. We can bring a moody attitude and have a depressing day. We can bring a grouchy attitude and irritate our coworkers and customers. Or we can bring a sunny, playful, cheerful attitude and have a great day. We can choose the kind of day we will have. We spent a lot of time talking about this choice, and we realized that as long as we are going to be at work, we might as well have the best day we can have. Make sense to you?"

"It sure does."

"In fact, we got so excited about our choices that we also chose to be world famous. A day spent 'being world famous' is a lot more enjoyable than a day spent being ordinary. Do you see what I'm saying? Working in a fish market is cold, wet, smelly, sloppy, difficult work. But we have a choice about our attitude while we are doing that work."

"Yes, I get it. You choose the attitude you bring to work each day. That choice determines the way you are

FISH!

at work. As long as you're here, why not choose to be world famous rather than ordinary? It seems so simple."

"Simple to understand, but more difficult to do. We didn't create this place overnight; it took almost a year. I was a hard case myself—you might say I used to have a chip on my shoulder. I mentioned that my personal life was kind of out of control as well. I really never thought much about it, just assumed I knew how life worked. Life was tough, and I responded in kind—I was tough. Then when we decided to create a different kind of fish market, I resisted the notion that I could choose how I lived each day. I had too much invested in being a victim. One of the older guys, who also had been through some tough times, took me aside and explained it to me, one monger to another. I did some soul searching and decided I would give it a try. I've become a believer. A person can choose his or her attitude. I know that because I chose mine."

Mary Jane found herself impressed with what she was hearing and also with the person from whom she was hearing it. She looked up to find Lonnie eyeing her quizzically and realized she had been daydreaming. "Sorry. I'll give it a try. What else explains your success here?"

"There are four ingredients, but this one is the core. Without choosing your attitude the others are a waste of time. So let's stop here and save the other three for later. Take the first ingredient and see what you can do with it back on the third floor. Call me when you're ready to discuss the rest. Do you have our number?"

"It's written everywhere in the shop!"

"Oh, yeah. We aren't shy, are we? See you later. And thanks for the yogurt."

The Courage to Change

The demands of her job kept Mary Jane on a treadmill of activity for the next two days. That was her excuse, anyway. But her thoughts were often on her conversation with Lonnie and the idea of choosing the attitude you bring to work. She realized that even though she agreed with the philosophy of the fish market, there was something holding her back. *When in doubt, get more data*, she thought.

On Friday, she decided to call Bill and ask him about the conference his boss had attended, the one about spirit in the workplace. It might be wise to learn more about his experience.

"Bill, how can I get up to speed on the 'spirit in the workplace' conference the big guy attended?"

"What do you want to do that for? It was one of those New Age deals. They probably spent most of their time in hot tubs. Why do you want to waste your time on that?"

FISH!

Mary Jane felt herself getting angry. She took a deep breath. "Look, Bill, when I took this job we both knew there was a lot to do. Now the stakes are higher, and the timeline is shorter. You're in this as deep as I am. Are you going to help me or give me a hard time?"

I can't believe I said that, she thought. *But it sure felt good!*

Bill responded evenly; this confrontational approach actually seemed to make him more comfortable. "OK, OK. Don't get all worked up. I have a CD from the conference on my desk that I'm supposed to listen to. I just haven't had time. You take it and fill me in?"

"Sure, Bill. I'll come by and pick it up."

A Memorable Commute

The commute to Bellevue that night was bumper-to-bumper, but Mary Jane didn't notice. She was mulling over her situation. *When did I lose my confidence?* she wondered to herself. *Speaking up to Bill is the first courageous thing I've done in a long time. Two years, to be exact*, she realized, as she finally started putting the pieces together at the edge of her consciousness. *Too much to think about.* Feeling overwhelmed, she decided to play Bill's CD.

FISH!

From the car stereo speakers came a deep, resonant voice that was mesmerizing. The CD opened with a recording of verse from a poet who took his poetry to the workplace, believing it could help us cope with the issues of the day. His name was David Whyte. He would talk a while and then recite a poem. His poems and stories washed over her. Phrases jumped out at her.

> The needs of the organization and our needs as workers are the same. Creativity, passion, flexibility, wholeheartedness...

Yes, she thought.
> We crack the windows of our cars in the corporate parking lot in the summer, not to save the upholstery from the heat, but because only sixty percent of us goes into that place, and the rest of us stays in the car all day and must breathe out there. What would it be like to take our whole self to work?

Who is this guy? Then without warning, she filled with emotion as she heard David Whyte recite his poem *Faith*. He introduced it to his audience by saying he wrote it at a time when he had very little faith himself:

FISH!

Faith

by David Whyte

I want to write about faith,
about the way the moon rises
   over cold snow, night after night,

faithful even as it fades from fullness,
   slowly becoming that last curving and impossible
     sliver of light before the final darkness.

But I have no faith myself
   I refuse it the smallest entry.

Let this then, my small poem,
   like a new moon, slender and barely open,
     be the first prayer that opens me to faith.

FISH!

So this is what is meant by the statement "When the student is ready the teacher appears." The poem had created a moment of insight, and Mary Jane finally saw what was holding her back. With Dan's sudden death and the pressures of being a responsible single mom, she had lost faith in her ability to survive in the world. She was afraid that if she took a risk and failed, she would not be able to support herself and her children.

Leading a change at work would be risky. She could fail and lose her job. That was a distinct possibility. Then she thought about the risk of not changing. *If we don't change, we could all lose our jobs. Not only that: I don't want to work in a place with no energy or life. I know what it will do to me over time, and the picture is not pretty. What kind of a mother would I be if I let that happen? What example would I set? If I launch the change process on Monday, the first step must be for me to choose* my *attitude. I choose faith. I must trust that whatever happens I will be all right.*

I'm a survivor; I've proven that. I will be all right, whatever happens. It's time to clean up the toxic energy dump. Not just because it would be good for business—although I believe it will be great for business. And not just because I have been challenged to solve the problem—that is an important reason, but it's an external issue. The compelling reason to move

FISH!

ahead comes from my inside. I need to renew my faith in myself; tackling this problem will help me do just that.

She remembered some lines from the reading: "I don't believe that companies are necessarily prisons, but sometimes we make prisons of them by the way we choose to work there. I have created a prison and the walls are my own lack of faith in myself."

The prison metaphor had a familiar ring—she was sure she had encountered it before in a seminar she had attended. As soon as she arrived at the day care to pick up Stacy, she parked her car, took out her journal, and dashed off her thoughts:

> Life is too precious to spend any time at all, much less half of my waking hours, in a toxic energy dump. I don't want to live like that, and I am sure my associates will feel the same way once they have a recognizable choice.
>
> The culture in my department has been the way it is for a long time. In order to change the culture, I will need to take personal risks with no assurance of success. This could be a blessing. Recent events have shaken my faith in myself, and taking the necessary risks could help me renew my faith. The fact is that the risk of

doing nothing is probably greater than the risk of acting.

Somewhere in my files is material containing a message that could be timely. I need to find that message because I need all the help I can get.

With that she got out of the car and went in to pick up her daughter.

"Mommy, Mommy. Your eyes are wet. Have you been crying? What's wrong, Mommy?"

"Yes, sweetheart, I've been crying, but it was good crying. How was your day?"

"I made a picture of our family; do you want to see it?"

"I sure do." She looked down and saw the four figures her daughter had drawn, looking back at her. "Oh, boy," she exhaled. *Another test of faith.*

"Get your things, honey; we have to go pick up Brad."

Sunday Afternoon

Sunday afternoon was Mom's time. Mary Jane arranged to have a sitter for at least two hours every Sunday. It was a little reward she gave herself, one that always left her refreshed and ready for the challenges of work and

FISH!

family. She used the time to read inspirational material or a good novel, go for a bike ride, or just sip coffee and relax. Seattle was full of coffee shops and there was a great spot three blocks away. She grabbed some books and headed out. Her favorite table in a private corner of the shop was waiting for her.

"Grande skinny latte, please." She sat down with her latte and decided to start with some inspirational reading. She pulled out her tattered copy of Sarah Ban Breathnach's *Simple Abundance*, a book that contains a reading for every day of the year, and turned to February 8. Key words seemed to jump off the page:

> Most of us are uncomfortable thinking of ourselves as artists...But each of us is an artist... With every *choice*, every day, you are *creating* a unique work of art. Something that only you can do...The reason you were born was to leave your own indelible mark on the world. This is your authenticity...*Respect* your creative urges...step out in *faith*...you will discover your *choices* are as authentic as you are. What is more, you will discover that your life is all it was meant to be: a joyous sonnet of thanksgiving.

FISH!

The words about choice and faith took Mary Jane back to the fish market. *Those guys are artists*, she thought, and *they must choose to create each day.* And she had a startling thought: *I can be an artist, too.*

Then, she took out a file from a leadership seminar she had attended years ago. This was where she first heard prison being used as a metaphor for work. Inside was a faded photocopy of a speech written by John Gardner. She recalled that Gardner encouraged people to reproduce his papers, a generous gesture, she thought. *He must have said something powerful if I remember him after all this time.* She searched through the speech, page by page.

The Writing of John Gardner

The passage began:

> There is the puzzle of why some men and women go to seed, while others remain vital to the very end of their days. Going to seed may be too vague an expression. Perhaps I should say that many people, somewhere along the line, stop learning and growing.

FISH!

Mary Jane looked up as she thought, *That fits my group. And it fits the old me, as well.* She smiled at the decision implied by "the old me." She went back to the passage:

> One must be compassionate in assessing the reasons. Perhaps life just presented them with tougher problems than they could solve. Perhaps something inflicted a major wound to their self-confidence or their self-esteem... Or maybe they just ran so hard for so long that they forgot what they were running for.
>
> I'm talking about people who, no matter how busy they may seem, have stopped learning and growing. I don't deride that. Life is hard. Sometimes just to keep on keeping on is an act of courage...
>
> We have to face the fact that most men and women out there in the world of work are more stale than they know, more bored than they would care to admit...
>
> A famous French writer said, "There are people whose clocks stop at a certain point in their lives." I've watched a lot of people move through life. As Yogi Berra says, "You can

FISH!

observe a lot by watching." *I am convinced that most people enjoy learning and growing, at any time in their life. If we are aware of the danger of going to seed we can take countervailing measures. If your clock is unwound you can wind it up again.*

There is something I know about you that you may not even know about yourself. You have within you more resources of energy than have ever been tapped, more talent than has ever been exploited, more strength than has ever been tested, and more to give than you have ever given.

No wonder I remember John Gardner. I have a lot of clocks to wind up, but first I need to wind up my own, she thought.

For the next hour Mary Jane wrote in her journal and was pleased to note that she had become quite peaceful. As she prepared to return home, she looked over what she had written and circled the section that would be her guide on Monday morning.

Solving the problem of the toxic energy dump will require me to become a leader in every sense of the word. I will need to risk the possibility of failure. There is no safe harbor. But to take

FISH!

no action is to fail for sure. I might as well get started. My first step is to choose my attitude. I choose confidence, trust, and faith. I will wind up my clock and get ready to enjoy learning and growing as I work to apply the lessons from the fish market to my toxic energy dump.

Monday Morning

At 5:30 A.M. she felt some pangs of guilt as she sat outside her daughter's day-care center, waiting for the doors to open. On rare days like this, Brad would also stay at the day care until a bus took him to school. She looked over at the sleepy-eyed kids and said, "I won't get you out of bed so early very often, kids, but today I need to get to the office to prepare for a really important project."

Brad rubbed his eyes and said, "That's all right, Mom." Then Stacy piped up, "Yeah, it's fun to get here first. We get first pick of video games!"

When the doors opened, Mary Jane signed them in and gave them each a big hug. When she looked back they were already busy.

It was an easy commute; by 5:55, she was at her desk with a steaming cup of coffee and a pad. She took out a pen and wrote in large letters:

FISH!

Choose Your Attitude

Steps:
- Call a meeting and speak from the heart.
- Find a message that communicates the notion of choosing your attitude in a way that everyone will understand and personalize.
- Provide motivation.
- Persist with faith.

Now the tough part. What do I say to my staff here on three? And she began writing down her thoughts.

On Monday mornings the staff met in two shifts; one group covered the phones while the other met with her in the conference room—then they switched. As the first group assembled, she listened to the discussions of family activities and the universal complaints about Monday morning. *These are good people*, she thought; she felt her heart beating faster as they quieted and turned their attention to her. *Here goes everything.*

Mary Jane's Presentation

"Today we have a serious issue to discuss. A couple of weeks ago the group vice president went to a conference and returned convinced that First Guarantee needs to become a place that is more energetic and enthusiastic. He is convinced that energy and enthusiasm are the keys to productivity, successful recruitment, long-term retention, great customer service, and a host of other qualities that we need in order to compete in our changing and consolidating business. He called a meeting of the leadership group—and at that meeting he referred to the third floor as a 'toxic energy dump.' That's right: he called our floor a toxic energy dump and said it needed to be cleaned."

Mary Jane looked at the startled expressions. A comment came quickly from Adam, a long-term employee: "I'd like to see them do this work. It's the most boring work on earth."

Then one of the least energetic employees said, "What difference does it make if there is energy here? We get the work done, don't we?"

No one challenged the accusation that their energy was toxic.

FISH!

Mary Jane continued, "I want you to know that this issue is not going away. Oh, the group VP may lose interest, and Bill might forget about it with time, but I will not. You see, I am in full agreement. We are a toxic energy dump. Other parts of the company hate dealing with us. They also call us 'the pit.' They joke about us at lunch. They laugh about us in the halls. And they're right. Heck, many of us hate coming here, and even we call this a pit. I think we can and should change that; I want you to know why."

The startled expressions were now replaced with truly stunned expressions. The silence was complete. "Many of you know my story. How Dan and I came to town with our hopes, dreams, and two small children. How Dan's sudden death left me alone. How Dan's insurance didn't cover many of the big expenses. How I found myself in a difficult financial position.

"What you may not know is how all this affected me. Some of you are single moms and dads and know what I'm talking about. I needed this job, and I had lost my confidence. I went with the flow, never doing anything that could threaten my security. Well, those days are over.

"Here is the bottom line. I still need this job, but

I don't want to spend the rest of my working life in a toxic energy dump. Dan's lesson had been lost on me until now. *Life is too precious just to be passing through to retirement.* We simply spend too much time at work to allow it to be wasted. I think we can make this a better place to work.

"Now, the good news. I know someone who works for a world-famous organization and is an expert on energy. You will meet him eventually. Today I'm going to convey his first bit of advice: *We choose our attitude.*"

Mary Jane continued by discussing the concept of choosing your attitude. Then she asked if there were any questions.

Steve raised his hand. When Mary Jane nodded to him, he said, "Suppose I'm driving my car and some idiot cuts me off in traffic. That causes me to get upset and I may honk or even make a gesture, if you know what I mean. What's with the choice thing? I didn't do it; it was done to me. I didn't have a choice."

"Let me ask you something, Steve. If you were in a tough part of town, would you have used that gesture?"

Steve smiled. "No way! You can get hurt doing that."

FISH!

"So you can choose your response in a tough part of town, but you have no choice in the suburbs?"

"OK, Mary Jane. OK, I get it."

"You couldn't have asked a better question, Steve. We can't control the way other people drive, but we can choose how we respond. Here at First Guarantee we don't have a lot to do with selecting the work that needs to be done, but we can choose how we approach that work. I want all of you to think of ways this is true and see if you can identify things we can do to remind ourselves of our choices. Good luck. Our work life depends on it." The second staff meeting was much like the first. When she didn't get any questions, she used Steve's question from the first group. It was 10:30 on Monday morning. She was drained from the meetings, but realized it was her first opportunity to choose her attitude.

And she did.

The week sped by. She made a point of walking around the office each day and being available to talk about the idea of choosing your attitude. When she saw Steve, he said, "Boy, you really nailed me at the staff meeting."

"I hope I didn't embarrass you."

FISH!

"Mary Jane, you did me a big favor. My life has been a series of reactions lately. You reminded me that I have important choices to make and that I can make them if I have a little self-control and courage."

"Courage?"

"I'm in a bad relationship; I need to do something about it. I can see now that reacting and feeling like a victim is not going to solve the problem. The problem needs to be confronted. I'm sorry to be so evasive, but it's rather personal."

"Good luck, Steve, and thanks for trusting me with your story."

"Oh, we all trust you, Mary Jane. It's just that this work is so boring and all we hear are complaints. We feel like we're always under attack. Keep at it; I'm behind you all the way."

She was pleasantly surprised by the many words of encouragement. While staff members were not sure about the details, most liked the idea of creating a more satisfying work environment.

Then on Friday it happened. She walked off the elevator on the third floor and was confronted with a giant poster. On the top it said: CHOOSE YOUR ATTITUDE, and in the middle were the words: MENU CHOICES FOR THE

FISH!

DAY. Down below the menu were two drawings. One was a smiling face and the other was a frowning face. She was ecstatic. *They do get it!* she thought to herself and raced to her office to call Lonnie.

After telling him about the menu, she suggested they meet for lunch on Monday to finish their discussion. Mary Jane said she really didn't want to wait until next week, so they agreed she should come to the market on Saturday and bring the kids with her.

Saturday at the Fish Market

Saturdays are always busy at the market, so Lonnie suggested they come early. Mary Jane foolishly asked what the earliest time was they might arrive. Lonnie said he started work at 5:00 A.M. They settled on 8:00.

Brad and Stacy got in the car drowsy, but by the time they had all made the trip into Seattle and found a parking spot, her kids were wired and ready for action. The questions were unending. "Where do they get the fish? Are they big fish? Do they have any sharks? Will there be any other kids there?"

As the three walked down Pike Place to the market, Mary Jane was struck by how quiet and calm it was.

FISH!

She immediately spotted Lonnie standing by the fish display. She was impressed with how neatly organized the stand was, with the fish and seafood packed in ice and signs detailing names, prices, and special qualities. One section was empty except for the ice.

"Good morning," said Lonnie with his customary smile. "And who are these two fishmongers?"

Mary Jane introduced her children. Lonnie welcomed them and said it was time to get to work. As she was removing her notepad from her purse, he stopped her and said, "No, not that kind of work. I thought you three could help me finish this display."

"Cool," said Brad.

"I couldn't find any boots your size, but I did find three aprons to wear. Here, put these on and we'll start packing fish."

Stacy looked a little bewildered; Mary Jane gave her a quick hug. Lonnie took Brad into the back of the store to visit the fish locker, while Mary Jane kept Stacy entertained with a walk among the displays. In about fifteen minutes, Lonnie and Brad returned, pushing a mammoth cart full of fish. To be exact, Lonnie was pushing the cart—Brad was hanging on to the handle with his feet just touching the ground.

FISH!

PLAY

"Mom! Wow! It rocks back there! There must be a million fish. Isn't that right, Lonnie? I got to help, too!" Lonnie gave him a big smile and a nod, but pretended to be all business. "We have to pack these fish so the market can open, little buddy. Ready to give me a hand?"

Brad was having a ball. He would help Lonnie pick up a tuna and Lonnie would pack it in ice, adding to a neat row of fish. The tuna were almost as big as Brad, and Mary Jane snapped a few great pictures with her smartphone. The way Lonnie worked with Brad was magic. Once in a while Lonnie would trick Brad, pretend the fish bit him, or do something that caused Brad to laugh. When there was room for only two more tuna in the row, Lonnie turned the job over to Brad, but provided some subtle help lifting. If Brad were asked to pick his "action hero" at that moment, he would have chosen Lonnie.

"Now it's time for your mom to get to work. Take out that notebook, Mary Jane, and Brad will give you the second ingredient of an energy-filled workplace."

"Brad?"

FISH!

"You bet. The second ingredient selected by a bunch of fishmongers who choose their attitude is something that is familiar to any kid. We just forget its importance as we become older and more serious. Brad, tell your mom what you do at recess."

Brad looked over the top of the tuna that was pinning him to the edge of the counter and said, "Play." Mary Jane opened her journal and made a new note: "PLAY!" Her mind flashed back to the scene at the market she witnessed on that first day. She had been looking at a playground with adult kids at recess. Throwing fish, kidding with each other and the customers, calling out orders, repeating the calls. The place had been electric.

"Don't misunderstand," said Lonnie. "This is a real business, which is run to make a profit. This business pays a lot of salaries, and we take the business seriously, but we discovered we could be serious about business and still have fun with the way we conducted it. You know, not get all uptight, but let things flow. What many of our customers think of as entertainment is just a bunch of adult kids having a good time, but doing it in a respectful manner.

"And the benefits are many. We sell a lot of fish.

FISH!

We have low turnover. We have become great friends, like the players on a winning team. We have a lot of pride in what we do and the way we do it. And we have become world famous. All from doing something that Brad does without much thought. We know how to play!"

Brad said, "Hey, Mom, why don't you bring the people at work to Lonnie so he can teach them how to play?"

MAKE THEIR DAY

Suddenly someone addressed Mary Jane, still taking notes, from the side. "Hey, reporter lady, want to buy a fish?" One of Lonnie's associates had come over and was holding a huge fish head in his hand. "I'll give you a great deal on this one. It's missing a few parts but the price is right." He made the fish's mouth into a smile and said, "I call it smiling sushi. Just a penny." And he looked at her with a crazy, crooked smile.

Lonnie was laughing and, of course, Brad wanted to hold it. Stacy was hiding behind Mom's legs. Mary Jane took out a penny and gave it to the fish guy they called "Wolf." She didn't need to ask why they called

FISH!

him Wolf. His hair was unruly and his eyes tracked everything as if it were prey. This wolf was clearly domesticated, however, and if such a thing were possible, Wolf had a grandfatherly air about him. Wolf put the smiling sushi in a bag and gave it to Brad, who was beaming. Shy Stacy piped up for the first time that morning and said she wanted one, too. Wolf brought over two more. Now they all had a smiling sushi.

Lonnie said, "Thanks, Wolf. You just showed us the third ingredient in creating a high-energy, world-famous market."

"He did?"

"Think back to the first two times you were here, Mary Jane. What stands out in your mind?"

"I remember a young redheaded woman, about twenty years old. She got up on the platform and tried to catch a fish. Of course she found them a little slippery and missed twice. But she had a ball."

"Why was that so memorable?"

"She was so animated, so alive. And the rest of us in the crowd identified with her. We could imagine ourselves in her place."

"And what do you think Brad will remember about today?"

"Doing big-guy stuff, visiting the cold fish locker, and working with you."

"We call that *make their day*. We look for as many ways as we can to create great memories. And we create great memories whenever we *make someone's day*. The playful way we do our work allows us to find creative ways to engage our customers. That's the key word: *engage*. We try not to stand apart from our customers but to find ways to respectfully include them in our fun. When we're successful, it makes their day."

Mary Jane opened her journal again and wrote: "MAKE THEIR DAY." Her mind filled with thoughts: *They engage people and welcome them to join in the fun. Customers like being a part of the show, and memories are created here that will bring smiles and make good stories for a long time afterward. Involving others and working to "make their day" directs attention toward the customer. Great psychology. Focusing your attention on ways to make another person's day provides a constant flow of positive feelings.*

"Hello, anyone home?"

Lonnie, Brad, and Stacy were all staring at her. "Sorry, I got to thinking about how powerful an ingredient that is. I hope we can find a way to apply *make their day* at First Guarantee."

FISH!

"The market is opening. Let's take the kids for something to eat; we can finish our discussion there. You kids hungry?"

"Yeah!"

BE THERE

They found a table at the café across the street and ordered coffee, hot chocolate, and sweet rolls. The market was rapidly filling with people, and Lonnie directed her attention to the way the fish guys interacted with those people. He asked her to watch them in action and told her she would discover the final ingredient if she watched carefully. Her eyes went from one monger to another, marveling at their playful manner and the lighthearted way they went about their work. She then turned her attention to those who were between activities. They looked vigilant, eyes roaming for the next opportunity for action.

It was actually a bad experience from the night before that helped her find the answer. She remembered her trip to the store with two cranky kids, both ready for bed. How long did she stand at the counter waiting for a clerk who was talking to another clerk about the modifications he made to his car? It seemed forever as the kids pulled on her dress with growing impatience. *That wouldn't happen here*, she thought. *These guys are present. They are fully engaged in their work. I wonder if they even daydream?* She asked Lonnie if that was the answer.

"You got it. Why am I not surprised?" He flashed his boyish grin. "Look out, toxic energy dump, here she comes!" Then Lonnie continued, "I was at the grocery store, waiting my turn at the meat counter. The staff was pleasant and having a good time. The problem was that they were having a good time with each other, not me. If they had included me in their fun, it would have been a whole different experience. They had most of it right but were missing the key ingredient. They weren't present and focused on me, the customer. They were internally focused."

She opened her journal and wrote: "BE THERE." Lonnie demonstrated his commitment to be there for his coworkers when he said, "I need to get back to work. The guys were more than willing to cover for me, but I don't want to overdo it. There is, however, one piece of advice I would like to offer before I leave."

"I'm all ears."

FISH!

"Well, I don't mean to tell you how to do your job, but I think it will be important for you to *find a way for your staff to discover the Fish Philosophy for themselves*. I'm not sure just telling them about the Fish Philosophy will do the trick. Brad had a good idea when he said you should bring them here."

"You and Brad make quite a team. In my rush to solve the problem, I could easily forget that the members of my staff need to have learning experiences of their own, and time to internalize the experience. Thanks so much—for everything. You made our day."

Brad couldn't stop talking on the way home; it was all Mary Jane could do to be there for him. One somewhat crazy idea found its way into her head. She grinned and tucked it away for Monday.

> *She told me and then I*
> *discovered it for myself.*
> Unknown

Sunday Afternoon

During her private time on Sunday afternoon, Mary Jane opened her journal and briefly expanded on her notes. *What shall I call these four ideas? They are more than steps or points. They are principles, but that doesn't go quite far enough. How about practices? A practice is more than a theory. It's something that you actually put into action, and the more you do it, the better you get at it. Yes, these are practices.*

CHOOSE YOUR ATTITUDE—I think we have a good start on this one. The menu idea the staff came up with was terrific; the first real sign of progress. Without choose your attitude, all the rest is a waste of time. I need to continue exploring and expanding our awareness of this ingredient.

PLAY—The fish market is an adult playground. If the fish guys can have that much fun selling fish, there is hope for us at First Guarantee.

MAKE THEIR DAY—Customers are encouraged to play also. The atmosphere is one of inclusion. Not at all like the boss I had in L.A. who talked to me like I was a tape recorder and never shared any of the interesting work.

BE THERE—The fish guys are fully in the now. They are not daydreaming or on the phone.

FISH!

> They are scanning the crowd and interacting with customers. They talk to me as if I was a long-lost friend, focusing on what I need.

Monday Morning

As she entered the elevator, she noticed Bill right behind her. *That will save me the trip to his office*, she thought. The car was crowded so they didn't converse, but when the door opened on her floor, she turned to Bill and handed her boss her bag, which had a distinct odor emanating from it. "A gift, Bill. It's called a smiling sushi." As the door closed she heard a loud, "Mary Jane!"

A few seconds after she was at her desk the phone rang. "Strange gift, Mary Jane," said Bill with the hint of a smile in his voice. She told him what she had done on Saturday. "Stay with it, Mary Jane. I don't know what a fish market has to do with First Guarantee, but if you can make me smile with the day I have ahead, you may be on to something."

When she hung up the phone, she was aware that her relationship with Bill was somehow different. *I don't think many on his staff stand up to him*, she thought.

FISH!

Strange as it seems, I believe he appreciates the fact that I have chosen not to be intimidated.

The Field Trip

At the first of her two Monday morning staff meetings Mary Jane got right to the point. "I'm impressed and heartened by how you have worked at finding ways to remind us all that we can choose our attitude each day. The Choose Your Attitude Menu was a great idea, and it's the talk of the building. It's fun at last to hear some positive comments. Now it's time to take the next step. There is something I want you all to experience, so we are going on a lunchtime field trip. This group will go on Wednesday, the other group on Thursday. Brown-bag lunches will be provided, so just bring yourselves.

"The field trip will be to a place many of you have visited before. We are going to the Pike Place Fish Market, where we will study energy in action. There are a bunch of guys there who have solved their version of our problem. It will be our task to see if we can understand and apply their secrets for success."

"I have a dental appointment." "I have plans for lunch that day." The voices of those around her rose

FISH!

with objections. She was surprised when she heard a strong voice—her own—say, "I expect you all to be there and to rearrange your plans to make that possible. This is important."

On Wednesday, the first group met in the lobby and headed for the market. "All I want you to do is observe the scene you are about to see." Mary Jane chuckled, "Be sure to keep your yogurt handy." Her use of the Yogi Berra quote, "You can observe a lot by watching," received one polite laugh. *Well, it's a start*, she thought.

The fish market was busy when they arrived, and they quickly dispersed. That made it hard for her to watch reactions, but she did notice a few of her staff obviously enjoying themselves. She saw John and Steve in close conversation with one of the fish guys and moved closer to observe. "When you are present with people you look right at them...just like being with your best friend...everything is going on around you but you're still taking care of just them," said the redheaded fish guy to John.

Good for John and Steve, she thought. *Great initiative*.

On Thursday the second group made the trip, most likely briefed by the first group. There were almost no questions, and the group was rather reserved until something special happened. Stephanie, a longtime employee, was asked if she wanted to go behind the counter and catch a fish. Although she had seemed quite shy at work, she accepted. Two fish slipped through her grasp, much to the delight of the crowd and the special amusement of her coworkers. On the third try, she made a dazzling bare-handed catch, which was followed by thunderous applause, catcalls, and whistles. She was hooked as the fish guys made her day.

Stephanie seemed to open the door for others. As the fish flew overhead, the gang from First Guarantee did a lot more than raise their yogurt cups in the air.

Friday Afternoon Meetings

On Friday afternoon, she met with each group separately. "Wouldn't it be neat to work in a place where you could have as much fun as the guys do at the Pike Place Fish Market?" she asked. There were a few nods and some smiles as the image of a flying fish passed through their minds. Stephanie had the biggest smile of all. Then reality set in.

In both groups, protest followed the initial smiles. "We don't sell fish!" Mark said. "We don't have anything

FISH!

to throw," added Beth. "It's a guy thing," contributed Ann. "Our work is boring," said another. One wisecracker said, "Let's throw our computers."

"You're right; this isn't a fish market; what we do is different. What I'm asking is: Are you interested in having a place to work that has as much energy as the world-famous Pike Place Fish Market? A place where you smile more often. A place where you have positive feelings about what you do and the way you do it. A place you look forward to being at each day. You've already demonstrated that in many ways we can choose our attitude. Are you interested in taking it further?"

Stephanie spoke up. "I like the people here; they're good people. But I hate coming to work. I can hardly breathe in this place. It's like a morgue. So I might as well admit it: I've been looking for another job. If we could find a way to create some life here, it would be a more satisfying place to work, and I would definitely consider staying."

"Thank you for your honesty and courage, Stephanie."

Steve added, "I want to make this place more fun."

Randy raised his hand.

"Yes, Randy?"

"You talked about your personal situation the other day, Mary Jane. I never heard a boss do that before and it got me thinking. I'm raising my son alone, and I need this job and the benefits that go with it. I don't like to make waves, but I'm sorry to admit I sometimes take out my frustrations on people in other departments. They seem to have it so good, while I'm trapped here in this pit. You've helped me realize that we make this place a pit by the way we act here. Well, if we can choose to make it a pit, then we can also choose something else. The thought of doing that has me really excited. If I can learn to have fun and be happy here, well, then I guess I can also learn to do that in other parts of my life."

"Thanks, Randy." She turned and looked directly at him with gratitude, adding, "I see a few heads nodding, and I know you've said something really important here today. You have touched me and others with your words from the heart. Thanks. Thank you for your contribution. Let's build a better workplace, a place we love to be in.

"On Monday we'll start incorporating the practices that comprise the Fish Philosophy. Between now and then, I want you to think about your personal experience at the fish market and write down any questions

FISH!

or ideas you have. When we get together next time, we can discuss how to proceed. Just let what you saw at the market stimulate your thinking."

The wisecracker popped up again, "Well, if we can't throw our computers, can't we at least throw the confetti from the shredder?" Laughter filled the room. *That feels good*, she thought.

Mary Jane then passed copies of an outline she had developed at the market and walked everyone through her personal observations. She encouraged her staff to remember and record their own thoughts over the weekend.

After the second meeting ended, Mary Jane retreated to her office and sat exhausted at her desk. *I gave them something to think about over the weekend. But will they?* Little did she know that half a dozen of her employees would find a reason to visit the market again that weekend, many of them with family and friends.

Mary Jane's Outline

The Four Practices

Choose Your Attitude—The fish guys are aware that they choose their attitude each day. One of the fish guys said, "When you are doing what you are doing, who are you being? Are you being impatient and bored, or are you being *world famous*? You are going to act differently if you are being world famous." Who do we want to be while we do our work?

Play—The fish guys have fun while they work, and fun is energizing and stimulates creativity. How could we have more fun and create more energy?

Make Their Day—The fish guys include the customers in their good time. They engage their customers in ways that create energy and goodwill. Who are our customers and how can we engage them in a way that will make their day? How could we make each other's days?

Be There—The fish guys are fully present at work, focused on what others need from them. What can they teach us about being there for each other and our customers?

**Please bring your thoughts
with you on Monday.**

MJR

FISH!

That Weekend at the Fish Market

"Teacher give you an assignment?"

Stephanie looked up and simultaneously saw a fish fly through the air and Lonnie's smiling face. "Hi. I guess you might say my boss gave me some homework."

"That wouldn't be Mary Jane, would it?"

"How did you know?" Her response was drowned out by a monger shouting, "Three tuna flying away to Paris," with a fake French accent. Lonnie seemed to hear her anyway. *No wonder they're so good at being present*, she thought. *They have to be if they want to hear anything above all this commotion.*

"I saw you here during the week with Mary Jane's group. You are also the first yogurt dude I remember catching a fish as long as I've been here."

"Really?"

"So how can I help you? You seem puzzled."

She looked down at her notes. "I think I understand *be there*, the way you are right now with me. And when I was catching the fish—well...I will never forget the way you made my day. Play is something that comes easy for me, and I see why having fun while you're working helps you do a better job. But *choose your*

FISH!

attitude is still a bit of a mystery. I mean, doesn't your attitude have a lot to do with the way you are treated and what happens to you?"

"I know just the person you need to ask about attitude: Wolf. Wolf was on his way to a career as a professional race car driver when he had a serious accident. Well, I'll let Wolf tell the story. We need to go back into the locker. Will you be warm enough?"

"Can we come, too?"

Stephanie looked to her left and saw Steve, Randy, and one very cute child. After introductions, they all went back to talk to Wolf, who told them how, while he was recovering from his accident, he learned to choose his attitude every day. His words made a deep impression on the three and they vowed to share them with their fellow workers at the Monday meeting.

Afterward, Steve had to take off, but Stephanie, Randy, and Randy's son went across the street to a café. The adults sipped coffee, while Randy's son ate a giant chocolate chip muffin.

"You know," said Stephanie, "we might as well clean up our toxic energy dump because there is no guarantee the next job will be any different. And think about it. How many bosses are there like Mary Jane? I really

FISH!

respect her. Think about what she's been through. I hear she even stood up to that jerk Bill Walsh. None of the other department managers ever stood up to that bully. I mean, that counts for something, doesn't it, Randy?"

"Stephanie, you're reading my mind. If these fish guys could do what they've done, the sky is the limit for us with a boss like Mary Jane. It isn't going to be easy. Some of our coworkers are as frightened as I used to be. They're skeptical because they're scared. Perhaps if we provide a positive example it will help. All I know is that things won't get better until we choose to make them better—and I want things to get better."

As Stephanie walked to her car she noticed Betty and her husband. She waved and then became aware of three other people from her office in the crowd. *Great!* she thought.

The Plan Unfolds

There was a buzz in the room as the first group assembled for the Monday morning meeting. Mary Jane opened the meeting by saying, "We're here to clean up what has been called a toxic energy dump. Today we'll see if we have any additional lessons from the market and then decide on our next steps. Did anyone think of anything during the weekend that we should consider before moving on?"

Stephanie and Randy jumped to their feet and took turns recalling their conversation with Wolf. Stephanie began.

"Wolf was really cool, although he was a little scary at first. I mean his voice is like a growl. Anyway, he told us his story of having a career as a professional race car driver torn away from him by a freak accident. He said he wallowed in pity for a while and then, when his girlfriend left him and friends stopped calling, he realized he had a basic choice to make. He could choose to live and to live fully, or he could let life slip away in a series of missed opportunities. He has been making the choice to live fully every day since. It was quite a story."

"My son was fascinated with Wolf," continued Randy. "Wolf really got me thinking about our situation here on three, and how much power we have over the kind of place we create. We could make three into a great place to work if we learn the lesson of Wolf. We must choose our attitude every day and choose it well."

FISH!

Steve nodded in agreement. "Hearing Wolf talk about his choices made me think about how I choose to talk about my work," he said. "I realized that I complain a lot but never do anything about it. It's like my words don't help me to accomplish anything. But words like make their day or be there remind me that I can make somebody's life better. It makes me feel good about my job, even if it's not perfect."

"That's a great observation, Steve," Mary Jane responded. "I have heard it said that if you want to change your culture, change your conversations. Lonnie told me that when the guys at the market started to talk in new ways about their work, they started to live that way too. The Fish Philosophy will give us a new common language. The more we talk about being there for each other, making each others' day, playing and choosing our attitudes, the less time we'll have for words that don't move us forward."

Mary Jane smiled appreciatively. "Thanks, Steve. Thank you, Randy. Thanks, Stephanie," she said. "It sounds like you were busy this weekend. And thanks for not asking for overtime!" After the laughter died down, Mary Jane asked, "Who else has something to offer that will help us understand these practices?" Forty-

FISH!

five minutes later, she decided to bring the discussion to a close. "Any ideas on where we go from here?"

"Why don't we form a team for each of the four practices?" said one of the newer employees.

There were a number of nods.

"All right," said Mary Jane. "Let me make sure the other half agrees with this approach. Why don't you sign up for the group you prefer; if the other group goes along, I will put everything in memo form and get it to you tomorrow. Is there anything else to discuss?"

At the end of the meeting she passed around a sign-up sheet and asked each of them to sign up for one of the four teams. The second group fully supported the idea of teams and seemed relieved to have a concrete plan of action.

The Teams Go to Work

The Play Team had a few too many volunteers, so Mary Jane did a little gentle negotiating. "I have a genuine Pike Place Fish Market T-shirt for the first three volunteers who will move from Play to Choose Your Attitude or Be There." Once the teams were balanced, she put together a memo with the general guidelines and expectations.

TEAM GUIDELINES

- Teams will have six weeks to meet, study their topic, collect additional information, and put together a presentation that will be made to the group as a whole at an off-site meeting.

- Each presentation must have some action items that we can consider for implementation.

- Teams will be responsible for setting their own meeting times and may use two hours of work time each week for team business. Arrangements must be made to cover the work of those at team meetings during business hours.

- Each team has a budget of $200 to be spent at its discretion.

- Teams will facilitate their own meetings.

- I will be available to troubleshoot if the team reaches an impasse, but I would rather the team work out its issues as a team.

Good luck! Let's create a place where we all want to work!

MJR

FISH!

Team Reports

Six weeks had passed since the teams started meeting, and Mary Jane was excited for each team to make their presentations today. She had asked Bill if people from other departments could handle essential functions for a morning, so the whole group could meet; Bill surprised her by offering to help personally as well as organize the coverage. "I don't know what you're doing," he said, "but I already sense a new level of energy on three. Keep up the good work and let me know if there is anything else I can do."

She was a bit nervous. Each of the teams had asked her to meet with them at least once, and she had done her best to be helpful and supportive without taking control. Although she had been asked for reading material and the use of a conference room in the last two weeks, none of the teams had requested more than that. She really didn't have a clue about the specifics of any of the four presentations. And today was the day they would go off-site to hear the team reports.

At nine in the morning, they all walked down to the Alexis Hotel as Bill and the other volunteers arrived to cover the office. "Good luck," he said.

They arrived at the Alexis and were directed to

FISH!

the Market Room. *Appropriate*, she thought. She had decided that the Choose Your Attitude Team should present last. She had explained to each team: "I want the ingredient that underlies all of the others to be the last thing we consider."

She felt a surge of emotion as she entered the meeting room. The room was a sea of color, music, and energy. Balloons were attached to each chair, and colorful flower arrangements brought the room to life. *They have responded to the challenge*, she thought. *Their clocks are wound up again.* The biggest surprise of the day was sitting in the back of the room in his full fishmonger outfit. It was Lonnie. She took the seat next to him as things began.

The Play Team

One of the members of the Play Team called the room to attention and asked the whole staff to come up front. As directions were given, everyone stood around rather awkwardly. "Our report is in the form of a game that we'll all play," said Betty, the Play Team spokesperson.

The Play Team had designed a game using a path of

FISH!

Team Reports

Six weeks had passed since the teams started meeting, and Mary Jane was excited for each team to make their presentations today. She had asked Bill if people from other departments could handle essential functions for a morning, so the whole group could meet; Bill surprised her by offering to help personally as well as organize the coverage. "I don't know what you're doing," he said, "but I already sense a new level of energy on three. Keep up the good work and let me know if there is anything else I can do."

She was a bit nervous. Each of the teams had asked her to meet with them at least once, and she had done her best to be helpful and supportive without taking control. Although she had been asked for reading material and the use of a conference room in the last two weeks, none of the teams had requested more than that. She really didn't have a clue about the specifics of any of the four presentations. And today was the day they would go off-site to hear the team reports.

At nine in the morning, they all walked down to the Alexis Hotel as Bill and the other volunteers arrived to cover the office. "Good luck," he said.

They arrived at the Alexis and were directed to

FISH!

the Market Room. *Appropriate*, she thought. She had decided that the Choose Your Attitude Team should present last. She had explained to each team: "I want the ingredient that underlies all of the others to be the last thing we consider."

She felt a surge of emotion as she entered the meeting room. The room was a sea of color, music, and energy. Balloons were attached to each chair, and colorful flower arrangements brought the room to life. *They have responded to the challenge*, she thought. *Their clocks are wound up again.* The biggest surprise of the day was sitting in the back of the room in his full fishmonger outfit. It was Lonnie. She took the seat next to him as things began.

The Play Team

One of the members of the Play Team called the room to attention and asked the whole staff to come up front. As directions were given, everyone stood around rather awkwardly. "Our report is in the form of a game that we'll all play," said Betty, the Play Team spokesperson.

The Play Team had designed a game using a path of

FISH!

circles cut from colored paper and arranged on the floor so you could step from one circle to the next as the music played. Each circle had written on it a key point from their report. When the music stopped, the person standing on a specific circle was asked to read the text on it. On each circle was either a benefit of play or an idea for how to implement it at work. *Great work*, thought Mary Jane.

Benefits of Play

- Happy people treat others well.
- Fun leads to creativity.
- The time passes quickly.
- Having a good time is healthy.
- Work becomes a reward and not just a way to rewards.

Implementing Play on the Third Floor

Post signs saying:
 THIS IS A PLAYGROUND.
 WATCH OUT FOR ADULT CHILDREN.

FISH!

- Start a joke-of-the-month contest with its own bulletin board.

- Add more color and make the environment more interesting.

- Add more life with plants and an aquarium.

- Have special events such as a lunchtime comedian.

- Provide small lights to turn on when it's time to lighten up a bit or when you have a good idea.

- Include instruction in creativity.

- Construct a designated creativity area called the Sand Box.

- Form an ongoing Play committee to keep the ideas flowing.

The Make Their Day Team

The Make Their Day Team was next. "Go out into the hall and have some coffee while we set up," was their first instruction. When everyone was called back into the room, the staff was divided into small groups with

FISH!

a member of the Make Their Day Team in each group. Stephanie described the assignment as everyone milled around.

"I want each group to take fifteen minutes to develop a list of strategies for supporting and enhancing the work of a key group of people: our internal customers. But first I want to introduce some data. These are the findings of a customer survey we sent out.

"Take a deep breath because you aren't going to like what you see." A slide went up. A wave of shock passed through the room; there was actually one audible gasp.

Results of Customer Survey

1. Our customers dread working with us. They call us "the sleepwalkers" because we seem positively sedated to them. They would prefer a good fight than the impersonal treatment they receive.

2. The work we do is adequate, but we rarely offer to extend ourselves in order to help them serve the external customer. We do our job, period, and no more.

FISH!

> 3. We often treat our customers as if they are interrupting us.
>
> 4. We frequently pass our customers around from one person to another without ever conveying an interest in solving the problem. We appear to be attempting to avoid responsibility.
>
> 5. Our customers joke about our response, or lack thereof, to a problem that arises after 4:00. They laugh about the stampede to the elevator at 4:30.
>
> 6. Our customers question our very commitment to the enterprise.
>
> 7. We are referred to as the "last stage of decline."
>
> 8. Discussions have started concerning the possibility of replacing our department with an outside contractor.

Stephanie said, "Our team was first shocked and then angered by these findings. Slowly we came to realize that the customers feel how they feel. No matter what excuses we offer or what kind of spin we put on it, it doesn't change how our internal customers feel.

That's the reality as they see it. The question is, what are we going to do about it?"

Another team member continued with considerable passion, "I don't think we realize how important our role is in the business of First Guarantee. Many people count on us, and they look bad when we drop the ball or drag our feet. The fact that many of us have other obligations and that we aren't very high on the compensation scale is not their problem. They're just trying to serve the customers who pay our salaries—and we're seen by them as an impediment to high-quality service."

Then Stephanie said, "We need your ideas and need them badly. Please help us to take a step away from the dump and toward making our customers' day. Each group has forty-five minutes to come up with as many ideas as possible. Please find a seat and get started. A member of our team will serve as scribe." There was barely a moment of silence before the groups began attacking the problem, still riding on the energy generated by the first presentation.

When the time had come, Stephanie announced, "Let's take a short break while the scribes integrate their notes." After ten minutes, she reconvened the staff to review the summary report.

BENEFITS OF MAKE THEIR DAY

- It is good for business.

- Serving our customers well will give us the satisfaction that comes to those who serve others. It will focus our attention away from our problems onto how we can make a positive difference to others. This is healthy, will feel good, and will unleash even more energy.

Implementing Make Their Day

- Stagger our hours so there is coverage from 7:00 A.M. until 6:00 P.M. This will be good for our customers (and may also be helpful to some of us who need different start times).

- Pull together some focus groups to study ways we can be of service to our customers. Should we have specialty groups, for instance, focusing on specific customer categories?

- Have a monthly and an annual award for service, based on the recommendation of our customers who said their day had been made.

- Implement a 360-degree feedback process that includes our customers.

FISH!

- Appoint a special task force dedicated to surprising and delighting our customers.

- Ask our key customers to "come out and play" once a month.

- Study what it would take to implement the "moment of truth" idea, which started at SAS, Scandinavian Airlines. We would try to make every transaction with our customers a positive transaction.

Mary Jane quietly rejoiced. *If they care this much, we can turn our department around. Stephanie is on fire and her group shows signs of catching the same enthusiasm. We can do it! I know we can!* Out of the corner of her eye she noticed that Lonnie had a pleased look on his face.

The Be There Team

The Be There Team took an entirely different approach, which offered a welcome change of pace. With soothing music playing in the background, one of the group members said, "Close your eyes and relax for a minute. Breathe deeply as I guide you through a number of

FISH!

visualizations that will help us be fully present." When she was finished, she said, "Now listen as members of our group offer some thoughts. Stay relaxed, try to even your breathing, and keep your eyes closed."

A number of inspirational readings followed. One of the readings went something like this:

> *The past is history*
> *The future is a mystery*
> *Today is a gift*
> *That is why we call it the present.*

John offered a personal story. "I was living a busy life," he said with sadness in his voice, "trying to make ends meet and working both sides against the middle. One day my daughter asked me to go to the park. I told her it was a wonderful idea, but I had a lot to do at that moment. I said she should wait until later, after I had a chance to catch up. But there always seemed to be some urgent and pressing work to do and the days passed. Days led to weeks and weeks to months." With a choking voice, he said that four years passed and he never did go to the park. His daughter is now fifteen and no longer interested in the park, nor, for that matter, in him.

John paused and took a deep breath. "I talked to one

FISH!

of the fish guys about being there, and I realized how infrequently I was really focused on what others needed from me at home or at work. The fish guy invited me to visit the market with the whole family. My daughter didn't want to go, but I finally wore her down and she came along. We had a good time, and I worked on being there for my children. When my wife took my son down the street to the toy store, I sat down with my daughter and told her how sorry I was that I really hadn't been there for her. I told her I hoped she could forgive me and that while I couldn't change the past, I let her know that I was now dedicated to being there for her. She said I wasn't that bad a dad—I just needed to lighten up a little. I've got a ways to go," he said, "but I'm improving. Being there could help me recover something I wasn't aware I had lost: a relationship with my daughter."

After John was finished, Lonnie whispered to Mary Jane, "The fish guy was Jacob. He has been higher than a kite ever since. He's a new guy, and it was his first taste of really helping someone."

Janet also became quite emotional when she described a coworker at her previous job. "This person kept trying to get my attention," she said, "but I was distracted by personal issues, and we never connected. Then all hell broke loose. It seems she was in way over her head and was covering up the lack of progress by issuing imaginary reports. By the time it all came to light, it was too late to correct. She lost her job, the company lost a client and a great deal of money, and I eventually lost my job because we were unable to replace the work. All of this could have been avoided if I had been there for a coworker who was reaching out for help."

Then Beth told a personal story of riding on a stationary bike in front of the TV while trying to catch up on some reading, when her son came in and sat down on the couch. She could tell he was distressed. "A mother knows these things," she said. "In the past I would have continued doing what I was doing while talking to him. But experience and a divorce have taught me that efficiency isn't always wise or nice with loved ones. So I turned off the TV, got off of the bicycle, set the magazines aside, and spent the next hour listening deeply as my son described the difficult time he was having just coping with life. I was really glad I made the choice to be there for him."

A few more members of the group told a mix of personal and business stories. Then they confirmed their commitment to being there for one another and for internal customers. "When you are being there you show consideration for the other person," one of the team members added. They also committed to being fully present when discussing an issue, whether with each other or a customer; they would truly listen and not allow themselves to be distracted. They encouraged one another to ask, "Is this a good time? Are you present?" To support one another in asking these questions they established a code phrase. "You seem distracted" was chosen as a cue to signal a possible "be there" issue. Everyone agreed to give it a try. And everyone also agreed never again to read or answer emails while talking on the phone with a colleague or customer.

The Choose Your Attitude Team

Last came the Choose Your Attitude Team. Their verbal report was brief and to the point. "Here are the benefits our team identified as a result of choosing your attitude.

"First, by accepting that you choose your attitude, you demonstrate a level of personal accountability and proactivity which will fill the third floor with energy, all by itself.

"Second, choosing your attitude and acting like a victim are mutually exclusive.

FISH!

"Third, we hope the attitude you choose is to bring your best self to work and to love the work you do. We may not be able to do exactly what we love at the present time, but any of us can choose to love what we do. We can bring our best qualities to our work—it is our choice. If we can accomplish this one thing, our work area will become an oasis of energy, flexibility, and creativity in a tough industry."

Implementing Choose Your Attitude

Margaret, the highly animated team spokesperson, suggested that the implementation plan for Choose Your Attitude was a highly personal one. "Many of us have lost sight of our ability to choose. We must be compassionate with each other but work together to nurture our ability to exercise free will. If you don't know you have choices or don't believe you have choices, you don't. There are people in our group who have had some very difficult life experiences. It will take some of us quite a while to be able to internalize this idea that we can choose our attitude."

Another team member continued, "We have identified two ways to implement Choose Your Attitude and have already taken some steps.

FISH!

"First, we've purchased for everyone copies of a little book titled *Personal Accountability: The Path to a Rewarding Work Life*. Our group will organize discussion groups after you have had a chance to read it. If that goes well, we will follow with discussions of *The Seven Habits of Highly Effective People*, and *The Road Less Traveled*. These are timeless books and I think you will find them interesting if you haven't already read them. All of these books can help us understand the concept of choosing an attitude.

"Second, we've prepared an attitude menu for everyone to use back at the office. You've seen a version of this before. We still don't know who put the first one on our office door, so we can't give credit. Now you have your personal menu for each day."

Mary Jane looked down at her attitude menu. It had two sides. On one side was a frowning face surrounded by words like *angry*, *disinterested*, and *bitter*. On the other side was a smiling face with words like *energetic*, *caring*, *vital*, *supportive*, and *creative*. At the top it said: THE CHOICE IS YOURS. It was a nice extension of the menu over the main door to the third floor. Mary Jane jumped up and set off to congratulate each member of her staff with Lonnie a few steps behind her, providing his own brand of encouragement. It was after lunch before she finished talking with each person. She now knew they were well on their way to cleaning up the toxic energy dump.

Lonnie walked Mary Jane back to First Guarantee. It wasn't surprising that they attracted a few stares: a businesswoman and a fishmonger in full regalia. What was surprising was how many knew Lonnie.

"So, your boss doesn't know about the job offer, does he?" said Lonnie. Two weeks earlier, Mary Jane had received an unexpected call from First Guarantee's main competitor, making an attempt to lure her away.

"I don't think so. I believe the recruiter talked to my old boss. The woman who recently left First Guarantee for a wonderful position in Portland. I haven't said anything at work."

"I couldn't understand your turning down such a lucrative offer, but now I see why. You're committed to this process, and you couldn't let these people down, could you?"

"That was part of it, Lonnie. But after working so hard to make First Guarantee more fun and a better place to work, why would I leave? The good times are just starting."

Sunday, February 7: The Coffee Shop One Year Later

Mary Jane opened her book, *Simple Abundance*, and turned to February 7.

This stuff is timeless, she thought. *A year ago I was sitting here, wondering how I would ever clean up the toxic energy dump. In fact, it was here that I realized I was part of the problem and needed to lead myself before I could lead the group.*

Those committee reports at the hotel were a great start. The staff had always been capable of much more—it just took

FISH!

some fish guys to bring those capabilities to light. The third floor is a different place now, and our new problem is all the people from around the company who want to work there. I guess the energy was there all the time.

And the Chairwoman's Award was such a nice surprise. I think the chairwoman was caught off guard when I asked for so many copies of the award. One for me, one for Bill, one for each employee in the department, and one for Lonnie and each of the other fish guys. I enjoy seeing it hanging above their cash register at the world famous Pike Place Fish Market and displayed prominently in Lonnie's living room.

She opened her journal to one of her favorite selections she had transcribed, a piece written by John Gardner on the meaning in life.

Meaning

Meaning is not something you stumble across, like the answer to a riddle or the prize in a treasure hunt. Meaning is something you build into your life. You build it out of your own past, out of your affections and loyalties, out of the experience of humankind as it is passed on to you, out of your own talent and understanding, out of the things you believe in, out of the things and people you

FISH!

love, out of the values for which you are willing to sacrifice something. The ingredients are there. You are the only one who can put them together into that pattern that will be your life. Let it be a life that has dignity and meaning for you. If it does, then the particular balance of success or failure is of less account.

John Gardner

Mary Jane was wiping tears from her eyes as she closed the journal where she kept her thoughts and inspirational "keepers."

"Lonnie, could I have a piece of that scone before you finish the whole darn thing?" Lonnie had been sitting quietly across from her, reading. He pushed the plate over to her. When she reached down for the scone, she found instead a small diamond engagement ring sitting in the large open mouth of a fish head. She looked up at Lonnie, who had a large question mark on his nervous face. Choking with laughter, she sputtered, "Oh, Lonnie! Yes! Yes, I will! But don't you ever stop playing?"

It had been a cold, dark, dreary day in Seattle on the outside—but quite the opposite on the inside:

FISH!

THE CHAIRWOMAN'S AWARD CEREMONY

The chairwoman came to the podium and looked out at the audience. She glanced down at her notes and then looked up again, saying, "I can't remember a prouder moment in my life than tonight. Something very special has happened at First Guarantee. In a backroom operation on the third floor, Mary Jane Ramirez and her team members rediscovered that satisfying, rewarding work can be a choice we make when we come through the door in the morning. It is as simple as asking, 'Is this going to be a good day?' And answering, 'Yes! I choose to make this a great day!'

"Long-term employees have the enthusiasm of new hires and what was thought to be routine work has been transformed into value-added activity. I understand that the ingredients for this transformation were discovered at a local fish market. The team on the third floor observed that if you could make a fish market a great place to work, you could choose to make any department of First Guarantee a great place to work.

"The ingredients of this transformation are inscribed on a plaque that has been hung in the front entrance of our headquarters building. It reads as follows":

OUR WORKPLACE

As you enter this place of work please *choose* to make today a great day. Your colleagues, customers, team members, and you yourself will be thankful. Find ways to *play*. We can be serious about our work without being serious about ourselves. Stay focused in order to *be there* when your customers and team members most need you. And should you feel your energy lapsing, try this surefire remedy: Find someone who needs a helping hand, a word of support, or a good ear—and *make their day*.

FISH!-ing Lessons

Now that you've read *FISH!*, the question is: How do I bring this into my life? Here are some fundamental lessons we have learned from people who have successfully applied this philosophy at work and home. We have also included four stories taken from real life that show each of the practices in action. In each story a light heart, a will to serve, a commitment to being present, and accepting personal responsibility for your choice of attitude have paved the way to personal or organizational transformation.

Who are you being? FISH! is not a set of rules or a checklist of steps to complete. It's a way of thinking, a lens that helps you see more clearly how to be the person you want to be. The practices of FISH! help you to be more aware of who you are "being" while you're doing what you're doing.

It starts with YOU. No one else can live FISH! for you. No matter what is happening around you, you alone are in charge of choosing how you want to live.

Your choice attracts others. When you live FISH!, you experience a positive change in your relationships and in

FISH!

yourself. Like-minded people will notice and ask, "What are you doing? How can I do it too?"

Your words create your world. The way you speak affects how you think and act. The FISH! practices offer a positive language that shifts your conversations, both internal and external, toward what you can do to make life better for each other.

Acknowledge each other. In communities that keep the spirit of FISH! alive, members recognize each other for living it. When you see a colleague living one or more of the practices with a customer or coworker, thank them for what they did and who they were being while they did it. You will Make Their Day and reinforce your mutual commitment to FISH! at the same time.

Lead by example. The most effective leaders today lead through their example. If you are a leader—and we all lead from different places—The FISH! Philosophy is a powerful way to practice servant leadership. If you want your team to live FISH!, first live it yourself.

FISH! is a way, not a day. When introducing FISH!, some organizations focus on Play first, and they think it has to be a day, such as Crazy Hat Day or Fun Fridays. Any activity that brings colleagues together in a spirit of camaraderie, appreciation, and fun is good; just don't forget about the rest of the week. You can find joy at work and make a positive difference even if you're *not* wearing a goofy tie.

The FISH! practices work together. The four practices are interconnected. Where you find one, you'll find the others. While each of the following stories highlights one practice, look to see how the other three practices also show up.

"This Wonderful Night"

When a school district adopted FISH! as its behavioral model, staff and students began to make each other's day in amazing ways.

As a behavior specialist, Tamarah often wondered, "We don't punish children who don't know how to read. We teach them. Why not do the same with their behavior?"

Tamarah, who worked for a large school district near New Orleans, Louisiana, knew that simply punishing students for misbehaving did not work, certainly not in the long run. It was far more effective to teach them replacement behaviors. But which ones worked best?

Then she found The FISH! Philosophy and recognized that it captured what a great school culture looks like. The four practices were easy to remember and easy to implement, whether you were in first grade or in high school. Concepts such as Make Their Day and Be There shifted a student's thinking from "What can I do for *me*?" to "What can I do for *others*?" Understanding that you actually could choose how you respond to a tough situation gave them a sense of control they had never felt before. It felt better to

FISH!

achieve something positive rather than avoid something negative.

The staff benefited, too. Tamarah shared FISH! with everyone from administration to the custodial staff, so the students received a consistent message wherever they were in school. Being there for kids strengthened relationships and built trust. Students who had never let anyone in before opened their hearts, and their minds followed. One day, an elementary student with a history of discipline problems told Tamarah, "I love FISH! You know why? It helps you hear me."

FISH! is an integral part of the district's formal behavior program, Positive Behavioral Interventions & Supports (PBIS). Each district using PBIS selects its own set of behavioral expectations to teach, reinforce and measure. For Tamarah's district, FISH! was the perfect choice.

Through PBIS, the staff promotes the four practices in every aspect of school life. At one elementary school, staff and students gather each morning to share examples of how they live FISH!—like the first-grader who refused a dare to steal from a classmate because "that wouldn't make his day." Students entering high school learn the four practices, along with decision making and stress management, so they understand how to be successful members of the school community. These lessons build "social competence" that students can use the rest of their lives.

Large posters in common areas such as classrooms, main hallways, and the cafeteria help define what FISH!

FISH!

behaviors look like in those areas. Teachers have written pamphlets on how to apply the four practices at the movies, at home, at the grocery store.

An essential part of the program is recognizing and reinforcing behavior in the moment. When staff members observe students putting a FISH! practice into action, they don't just say, "Good job." They look them in the eye and tell them specifically what they did and how it fits with the way staff and students are choosing to live.

The results speak for themselves. For one, Tamarah's district has seen a dramatic decrease in tardies. One school went from hundreds of tardies during a certain period to just seven. Discipline problems have also decreased. Tamarah looked at research showing that without a systematic approach, teachers lose seventy-one days a year to behavior problems—stopping class, redirecting students, sending students to the office. By teaching more effective behaviors, Tamarah's district gained back many of those precious days, boosting learning.

The district also applied FISH! to its anti-bullying initiative. Its mantra is that bullying flourishes when good people do nothing. Bullying isn't just about bully and victim, it's about the bystanders who let it happen. The approach emphasizes that, "We have to Be There for each other and say, 'This is not OK." As empathy has grown, bullying has plummeted.

This thoughtful, caring spirit culminated in a memorable moment during homecoming week. On their own, the students at one high school in the district started a campaign to elect a new queen. They did not vote for the most popular student or the most athletic. They focused on a more meaningful quality—the student they felt best exemplified The FISH! Philosophy.

The night of the coronation, the football stadium was packed, standing room only. The crowd buzzed with anticipation as the members of the royal court were introduced. Finally it was time to announce the queen. This was always a big moment, but this year the atmosphere was charged with excitement. As the crown was placed on the student's head, the stadium thundered with cheers for their queen—a student with cerebral palsy, known for overcoming the many challenges in her life with an amazing spirit. As she beamed with pride, many in the crowd cried with joy.

The high school principal told Tamarah how proud he was of the students and how glad he was to be part of this amazing celebration. When she had first proposed The FISH! Philosophy as the school's behavioral model, he had been skeptical, he told her. "But now, I believe so much in what we do here. This wonderful night happened because of the culture we have developed in our school."

"A Make Their Day culture," Tamarah added, as she smiled and wiped a few tears from her eyes.

"Every Day Is a Gift"

You don't always have a choice about the challenges you face, Inge learned, but you do get to choose the attitude you bring to them.

For too long Inge had ignored some unpleasant physical symptoms, dismissing them as stress from her demanding sales job. But a visit to her doctor and a battery of tests revealed something life-threatening: a large mass, almost certainly cancer, that must be removed quickly.

When Inge met with her surgeon, he explained the risks and recommended that she "get her affairs in order."

"What do you mean?" Inge asked. She paused for several seconds. "All the way to the funeral?"

"Yes," the doctor said quietly.

Stunned and numb, Inge spent the next week writing letters to her children and making funeral preparations.

Later in the week, as she was driving to the funeral home to finalize her plans, she suddenly remembered a recent conversation with her close friend. "We've been talking at work about something called The FISH! Philosophy," her friend had said. *Strange name*, Inge thought. But

FISH!

as her friend went on to explain what FISH! was all about, two concepts caught her attention: Be There and Choose Your Attitude.

As Inge drove, she recognized what she must do. She decided to choose, consciously and intentionally, the attitude she would apply to the rest of her uncertain future. She turned the car around and drove home with a clear sense of purpose.

Inge decided to rename her cancer "the Glob" and asked everyone around her to call it that, too. She did not know if she could beat cancer, but she knew she could take on a glob.

The morning of her surgery, Inge woke up energized. She called the funeral home and left a message to cancel plans for her funeral. "I've changed my mind and I'm not coming," she said.

When Inge arrived at the operating room, she asked to meet with the surgical team. "I know you have seen what I have seen, and you have heard what I have heard, that I may very well die on the table," she told them. "But my daughter is graduating with a double master's degree with honors at the end of June. I am a single parent and I have to Be There for her. Also she is getting married in September and I have promised to walk her down the aisle and I am not backing out of it.

"I am asking you to not permit any negativity in this room. I am asking for energy. I am asking for laughter and a few prayers. I am asking you to operate on me with the attitude of improving my life. When you look at me during surgery, please see a lady who is walking her daughter down the aisle."

Then Inge gave them a CD she had made with her favorite high-energy rock-and-roll songs. The last thing she heard before she went under was "Tutti Frutti" and a nurse laughing.

When Inge woke up, a nurse asked with a big smile if she was OK. "Of course I'm OK," Inge said softly before drifting back to a deep, healing sleep. Inge's surgeon stopped by her room a few hours later and she thanked him for doing a great job. He responded by telling her that he was confident that he had removed all of "the Glob" and her prognosis was very favorable. He told Inge how the music had kept everyone on their toes, and how energetic and positive the staff had been.

Inge told him to keep the CD. "I've tried this cancer thing, and it wasn't a lot of fun, so I won't be doing it again," she said, laughing.

The surgeon laughed, too. He told Inge no one had ever spoken to his staff like she had and that it had made a difference. Inge asked the surgeon if he would deliver a similar message to his team before future surgeries, and he agreed. A year later, when she saw the surgeon for a follow-up, he said he was still using the CD and had created other upbeat soundtracks to play during operations.

FISH!

Life—and cancer—comes with no guarantees, even with the most positive attitude. Inge chose how she approached what she *could* control. It might not have increased the surgical team's medical skills, but it *did* affect how they applied the skills they already possessed.

According to Inge, "the Glob" woke her up. It helped her see life in a new way. Each person is a gift and each day is a gift, she told herself. No longer did she take anything for granted. She decided to Play, to have fun. She always did her best to Be There and, without hesitation, to Choose Her Attitude. "It makes each day better and keeps me aware of all the great people and blessings around me," Inge says. "It makes me and those around me happy."

"Thank You for What You Said"

An aunt in a hurry, a bookstore clerk on autopilot, and a guy who loves to talk about FISH! combine for a valuable Be There lesson.

Harry Geist loves to talk about The FISH! Philosophy. That's understandable, since his job at ChartHouse Learning is to help teams bring FISH! into their work.

But FISH! is much more than a job to Harry. He's always been a caring guy, but the practices have changed the way he treats others. When Harry is at a store or restaurant, he always introduces himself to the person who is helping him and asks their name. He uses their name for the rest of his visit and, without fail, sincerely thanks them for their efforts.

Once, on a business trip to Los Angeles with ChartHouse CEO John Christensen, Harry introduced himself to the bellhop showing him to his room. As usual he asked the man his name and expressed his gratitude. A few days later, as Harry and John were about to leave, John struck up a conversation with the bellhop in the lobby. "You must see a lot of movie stars at this hotel," John said.

FISH!

"Yes," the bellhop responded, listing several big names. "But of all the guests I've served, I remember your friend Harry the most. He's the only one who ever asked my name."

Because Harry is so tuned in to the importance of being there, he notices when someone *isn't* very present. One day, Harry went to a large chain bookstore to pick up a book he had ordered. While he was in line at the help desk, he overheard a woman tell the clerk in a hurried voice, "I'm looking for a book I loved as a girl and I'd like to buy it for my niece. I'm sorry to sound so rushed, but it's her birthday today and I'm running late for her party."

The man barely looked up as he asked in a monotone, "What's the name of the book?" The woman gave him the title and he typed it into the computer. A few moments later he said, "We don't have it in stock."

"Can you recommend anything else?" the woman said, sounding increasingly frazzled.

The man pointed to the back of the store and said flatly, "We have a children's book section."

The woman stormed off, heading for the exit, but not before muttering sarcastically, "Thanks for the help." The clerk seemed oblivious to this as he called, "Next."

The clerk wasn't exactly rude, Harry thought. But he wasn't exactly being present, either. Maybe the guy was just having a bad day. OK, but that doesn't mean you pass your unhappiness to the customer. Maybe he was bored. Again, not the customer's fault. Maybe I could help him, Harry wondered. For the next few minutes, he debated whether he

FISH!

should offer the clerk some "Be There" advice and contemplated what he would say if he did.

When Harry reached the front of the line, he asked for the book he had ordered and the clerk handed it to him. For a second Harry thought about leaving, but then he said, as politely as he could, "Do you mind if I offer you some constructive feedback?"

The clerk was a bit taken aback but said, "Sure."

"You know, that woman who was looking for the book for her niece?"

"Yeah, I looked it up but it wasn't in the store," the clerk said, a little defensively.

"I understand. But imagine if you had really been there for her. You might have said something like, 'Unfortunately we don't have the book in right now, but I've got an idea. Why don't you tell me a little bit about the book, and how old your niece is? Then we'll pick out three or four options together on the computer. I know you're late for the party, so I'll get some help to quickly pull the books for you. I bet we'll find something great for your niece.'

"Or, if you couldn't find a different book, how about brainstorming another way to solve her problem? Like putting a bookmark in a gift bag with a note about the 'special book' that will arrive in the mail in a few days. The woman probably would have gone to her niece's birthday party and told a great story about you and this store. As it is, she's probably never coming back."

The clerk stood there, mouth open. "Well, thanks for

FISH!

listening," Harry said as he walked away, wondering if he had made any difference. He browsed for another twenty minutes, and as he was heading for the door, he felt a hand on his shoulder. It was the clerk. He shook Harry's hand and said sincerely, "Thank you for what you said. You've helped me to see things I've never seen before in my work."

As Harry drove home, he thought about why being there is so important. You may deal with the same type of transaction or interaction over and over, but each one is unique. Why? Because every customer—and what they need from you—is unique. If the bookstore clerk had seen the woman as an aunt seeking a special gift for her niece, he would have been more likely to choose a more helpful attitude. That would have led him to playfully and creatively help the woman solve her problem, which would have made her day.

Harry often explains to people who are new to FISH! that this is what the philosophy does: It helps you see opportunities to help others that you never saw before.

"Smiles of Delight"

When the staff of Blue Care, a nursing care organization, applied a playful, innovative approach to a difficult, emotional care challenge, the results were dramatic.

It's not often that a nursing care organization is mentioned in the same company as pop music legends the Bee Gees, the Great Barrier Reef, country music star Keith Urban, golfer Greg Norman, and the famous song "Waltzing Matilda." Yet Blue Care joined this renowned group when the citizens of Queensland, Australia, voted it one of the 150 "icons" that have shaped the state's history and development.

Blue Care—named for the blue uniforms its nurses wore—earned its reputation by skillfully and lovingly delivering home care to seniors, people with disabilities, and others in need throughout Queensland, an area two and a half times the size of Texas. Today Blue Care is one of Australia's leading not-for-profit providers of community care, senior residential care, and retirement living.

Blue Care has created a care model that "tailors" how it delivers its many services to the unique needs of each

FISH!

individual. Because such flexibility requires high levels of teamwork and communication, Blue Care turned to The FISH! Philosophy. Steve Lundin has trained many of the staff, and FISH! is used as the language and approach that supports its care model.

It's easy to see how practices such as Be There, Make Their Day, and Choose Your Attitude fit with Blue Care's commitment to compassion, justice, respect, and working together. But the idea of Play—and playing with new ideas to improve care—also has made a powerful difference.

Several of Blue Care's residential care facilities have used an innovative approach to deal with the difficult and emotional challenge of caring for people with dementia. During a twelve-week pilot program, performers from a group called Play Up regularly visited the facilities. Steve saw the impact Play Up had firsthand, during one of his visits to Blue Care. Actors dressed in fun costumes stood in the middle of a room. They were surrounded by residents sitting on chairs and couches, many of them staring into space or sleeping.

With a variety of tools, from balloons to musical instruments, the actors engaged the residents in a caring and gentle way, but with playful energy. Some of the residents responded immediately by singing or dancing. Others, their dementia more advanced, were slower to get involved, but after just fifteen minutes Steve could see the effect on every person there. They had come alive.

FISH!

After the conclusion of the pilot program, staff analyzed the mood charts of fifty residents. They all showed the residents felt happier after each session of Play Up. Further, Blue Care found thirty-six percent of residents with a history of falling had fewer falls. And the use of antipsychotic medication at one of Blue Care's largest sites decreased fifty-two percent in the five months after Play Up compared to the five months before.

Along with the research, Steve has heard several anecdotal accounts of the success of the program. A resident who hardly spoke blossomed over the twelve weeks of the pilot, starting with one or two words. Before long she was greeting the performers and conversing with them. Another resident who roamed the halls, not interacting with anyone, sang and danced with the performers, a smile of delight on her face.

The program also helped the staff. When surveyed, staff members reported that Play Up had significantly improved their confidence to communicate, build relationships, and engage in pleasant activities and conversation with residents. The staff felt they had more confidence to create fun atmospheres, not only with the residents, but also among coworkers. Though staff indicated that the workplace could be stressful, after the program they felt their work at Blue Care had meaning and purpose, they were more enthusiastic, and their workplace had a positive atmosphere.

Play is an essential part of living and learning at all

FISH!

ages. Blue Care believes in "late-life" development, and that people with dementia can still find joy and reawakened expression through playful experiences. Playing and experimenting with new approaches helps the staff of Blue Care find innovative answers to the unique needs of its clients.

Play helps all of us to live to our full potential.

Acknowledgments

There are many who have worked very hard to make this book a success, and we want to recognize them all, fully knowing we will probably miss someone. First we will acknowledge the special people and then single out three for extra recognition.

You couldn't ask for a better publisher. It seems unfair to the industry that Hyperion should have so much superior talent. Included on the fantastic team with whom we had the privilege to work are Bob Miller, Martha Levin, Ellen Archer, Jane Comins, Michael Burkin, Mark Chait, Jennifer Landers, Claire Ellis, Andrea Ho, David Lott, Vincent Stanley, and Christine Pride, and special thanks to the awesome Hachette Book Group's sales force.

And how did we get so lucky as to find the world's best literary agency? The Margret McBride Agency includes an all-star cast: Jason Cabassi, Donna DeGutis, Sangeeta Mehta, Kris Sauer, and Faye Atchinson.

There would not be a book if it weren't for the incredible World Famous Pike Place Fish Market. Thanks to Johnny Yokoyama, the owner, and the amazing fishmongers for creating and sustaining a world-famous fish market.

FISH!

We are indebted to ChartHouse Learning for the many little gestures that add up to a whole lot of help, especially Harry Geist for his valuable insights and Patrick North and Jackie Johnson for their excellent design, with a special shout-out to wordsmith extraordinaire Phil Strand for his skilled and thoughtful writing of the new stories and material in this edition.

Thanks to our wives, Janell, Mary, and Gaye, for always being there and putting up with us.

And we would like to recognize three people who made major contributions:

Our editor, Will Schwalbe, brought enthusiasm, experience, and a willingness always to be looking for ways to improve the book, right down to the last minute.

Ken Blanchard offered his sage guidance and wrote a wonderful foreword.

Finally, the agent of all agents, Margret McBride: for a writer, she is a treasure.

Thanks.

Stephen C. Lundin

Harry Paul

John Christensen

About the Authors

Stephen Lundin brings to his work the experience he has accumulated while taking The FISH! Philosophy to organizations in 56 countries. He now limits his travel, focuses on the nonprofit world, and favors organizations that work with the elderly or the vulnerable. He enjoys providing talks and seminars to those with a core goal of better service to customers and who are dedicated to the idea that quality of work life matters. Contact Stephen C. Lundin at slrunner@aol.com.

Harry Paul travels the world presenting ideas and concepts from his books through energized and upbeat keynotes and seminars. He delivers programs based on **FISH!** *A Proven Way to Boost Morale and Improve Results*, **Who Kidnapped Excellence?** *What Stops Us from Giving and Being Our Best*, and **Instant Turnaround!** *Getting People Excited About Coming to Work and Working Hard.* For more information on having Harry present at your company or organization, visit his website at www.harrythefishguy.com; email him at thepauls@cox.net; or call (760) 212-8993.

As creator of The FISH! Philosophy, John Christensen leads ChartHouse Learning in the development of learning

FISH!

tools that help people to reach their full potential through the four practices. John and his team have filmed in many workplaces where FISH! lives, creating special programs for schools, health care and leadership, and to help teams keep the energy of FISH! alive. John has spoken to many organizations about how any team can use the four practices to transform their lives at work. Contact John at jc@charthouse.com.

These resources will help you bring The FISH!® Philosophy to life

FISH!® Showing *FISH!*, the film that started it all, to your group is an engaging way to ignite energy and spark essential conversations that lead you to improve customer service and increase employee retention. That's why this film, about real people who found a better way to work, is the best-selling corporate training video ever.

FISH!® Training FISH! helps people succeed in a team environment. Not all teams are alike, so we developed solutions for a variety of needs, including keynote lectures, in-house seminars, Train-the-Trainer, and customized live coaching webinars. We create engaging experiences that provoke culture-transforming actions.

FISH!® Interactive Learning This individual FISH! e-learning experience helps you apply the four practices in a way that is effective, memorable, practical, and convenient. FISH! Interactive Learning ensures that you will be "team ready"—a contributor everyone wants on his or her team.

For more on these and other FISH!® resources, contact www.FishPhilosophy.com or call (800) 328-3789.

≈ FISH! TALES ≈

The follow-up to *FISH!*, this best-seller offers inspiring stories of real people who applied The FISH! Philosophy to build trust and create remarkable business and personal results. It's packed with leadership lessons.

≈ FISH! STICKS ≈

How do you keep a team's vision, teamwork, and commitment strong when the inevitable pull of old habits resurfaces? This brilliant parable offers three simple ways to sustain positive change.

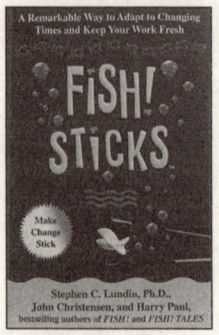

≈ FISH! FOR LIFE ≈

If The FISH! Philosophy is effective at work, why not apply it to daily challenges at home? A touching and practical story about being there for family, in good times and bad.

FishPhilosophy.com
HyperionBooks.com

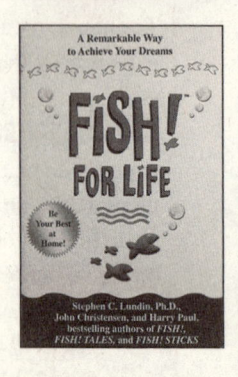

At bookstores now
HYPERION

FISH!

Choose Your Attitude ✦ Play ✦ Make Their Day ✦ Be There

Keep up with the latest happenings of all things FISH!

www.FISHtheBook.com

Be a part of the community, keep up with the latest happenings, and access all the resources you need to help you keep the spirit of FISH! alive.

Download an outline of how to use FISH! in your team training or a study guide for your reading group. Read more stories of how people are applying the practices. Watch videos with helpful insights on living the philosophy.

We also want to hear from you. If you have a story of your own about how the practices of FISH! have made a difference in your life at work or home, we'd love to hear it. Just send it to story@fishthebook.com.

FISH!

atch the Energy. Release the Potential.